CHURCH
Evangelism

CHURCH
Evangelism

BASIC PRINCIPLES • DIVERSE MODELS

John Mark Terry

BROADMAN
&HOLMAN
PUBLISHERS

Nashville, Tennessee

© 1997
by John Mark Terry
All rights reserved
Printed in the United States of America

0-8054-1065-1

Published by Broadman & Holman Publishers, Nashville, Tennessee
Acquisitions and Development Editor: John Landers
Page Design and Typography: TF Designs, Mt. Juliet, Tennessee

Dewey Decimal Classification: 250
Subject Heading: EVANGELISTIC WORK / CHURCH GROWTH
Library of Congress Card Catalog Number: 96-9145

Unless otherwise stated, all Scripture citation is from the Holy Bible, New International Version, copyright © 1973, 1978, 1984 by International Bible Society.

Library of Congress Cataloging-in-Publication Data
Terry, John Mark, 1949–
    Church evangelism : creating a culture for growth in your congregation / John Mark Terry.
        p. cm.
    Includes bibliographical references.
    ISBN 0-8054-1065-1
    1. Evangelistic work. I. Title.
    BV3790.T45 1997
    269'.2–dc20

96-9145
CIP

97 98 99 00 01 5 4 3 2 1

To Barbara
MY SWEETHEART,
LIFE'S COMPANION, AND BEST FRIEND

CONTENTS

❯——————————❮

PREFACE

————————————

Two startling facts prompted me to write this book. First, 80 percent of the Protestant churches in North America are plateaued or declining in number. This is a frightening statistic. If this trend continues, our churches will soon resemble the churches of Western Europe—beautiful edifices that are almost empty on Sundays. Clearly, our churches need to make changes and do things differently. In this book I will suggest several ways to do things differently or at least more effectively.

Second, in my own Southern Baptist denomination, thousands of churches baptize no one in a given year and thousands of others baptize only a handful. Southern Baptists have a reputation for being evangelistic. If this is true for Southern Baptists, what is the situation in other denominations? Obviously, we talk a better game than we play. I pray this book will provide church leaders with the information they need to make their churches more effective in evangelism.

I wrote this book with seminary students in mind. While there are many church evangelism books, few are designed as seminary textbooks. I hope teachers of seminary and Bible college courses on church evangelism will find this book useful.

I am grateful to several people who aided the production of this book. First, I'm grateful to my wife, Barbara, and to my children,

Joanna and Micah, for their patience. I had to go to the office on many Saturdays in order to complete the manuscript. I'm also grateful to Thom Rainer, dean of the Billy Graham School at The Southern Baptist Theological Seminary, for his advice and encouragement. Finally, I am grateful to my editor, John Landers, for his counsel, patience, and assistance.

Chapter 1

Accept the Biblical Mandate

❯——————❮

Evangelism reflects the essential nature of God. God is by nature loving and gracious. Because of his love and grace, God desires to redeem sinful humanity and thus reconcile all the world's people to himself. Genesis 3 tells how Adam and Eve rebelled against God. God could have struck dead the rebellious couple, but, instead, he sought them in the garden and provided garments for them. The Book of Revelation closes with an evangelistic invitation: "The Spirit and the bride say, 'Come!' And let him who hears say, 'Come!' Whoever is thirsty, let him come; and whoever wishes, let him take the free gift of the water of life" (Rev. 22:17). Truly, a "scarlet thread of redemption" runs through the Bible. God's essential nature prompts him to seek and save everyone who is alienated from him.

Godly churches, godly pastors, and godly Christians should all manifest the nature of their heavenly Father. If God reveals himself to be loving and gracious, then Christians and churches should be loving and gracious. Instead of condemning and rejecting people we, like God, should seek out the sinful and alienated and lead them to reconciliation with God. As Christians, we are responsible and privileged to do so. The church should announce that God has reconciled the world to himself through Jesus Christ because God has called the church to this "ministry of reconciliation" (2 Cor. 5:18–19).

In 2 Corinthians 5 Paul spoke of Christians as Christ's ambassadors in the world. The responsibility of ambassadors is to negotiate peace treaties. Like ambassadors, Christians seek to reconcile alienated sinners to God so they can experience peace with him. If Christians are like ambassadors, then churches are like embassies. They represent the interests of God and the citizens of his kingdom in the world.

All embassies have an immigration office that is responsible for providing information to those who desire to become citizens of the country sponsoring the embassy. This is a major function of a local church—to help people become citizens of heaven. If the church neglects doing this, it is a poor embassy indeed. Helping people become citizens of God's kingdom is the work of evangelism.

WHAT IS EVANGELISM?

If you are going to lead your church to do evangelism, you ought to know what the word means. The English word *evangelism* comes from the Greek word, *euaggelidzo,* which is often translated in English Bibles as "preach the gospel." *Euaggelidzo* comes from the word *euaggelion,* which means "gospel." Thus "evangelize" literally means "to gospelize." These two Greek words occur in the New Testament 127 times. Jesus himself told the people that he had to evangelize other cities (Luke 4:43). In his epistles, Paul spoke of his ministry as *evangelizing* twenty-three times. The frequency with which these words are used in the New Testament ought to say something to us about the priority of evangelism in our churches today.

There are many modern definitions of evangelism, perhaps because there are many books about evangelism. Still, the way you define *evangelism* is important because your definition says a lot about the way you will evangelize. For example, in recent years the World Council of Churches has defined *evangelism* as *presence.* This definition supports the notion that just maintaining a church or Christian institution is in itself evangelism. As you might expect, the World Council of Churches has continued to place less and less importance on sharing a spoken witness.

John R. W. Stott and others have defined *evangelism* in terms of *proclamation*. They believe that the church's responsibility is to proclaim the gospel clearly and then leave the results to God. The church growth movement has emphasized *persuasion*. Proponents of this movement believe that Christians should do everything ethically possible to persuade people to accept Christ. As you read the conceptions of evangelism printed below, you will recognize the different approaches mentioned above.

Delos Miles lists six conceptions of evangelism found in the writings of Christian theologians:

1. Bearing witness to the Lord Jesus Christ (witnessing)
2. Converting persons to the Lord Jesus Christ (soul-winning)
3. Proclaiming the Lord Jesus Christ (proclamation)
4. Making disciples for the Lord Jesus Christ (discipleship)
5. Planting and growing churches for the Lord Jesus Christ (church growth)
6. Initiating persons into the kingdom of God (Christian initiation)[1]

These concepts are helpful, but they are not formal definitions. Here are some popular definitions. You may find it helpful to write your own. Your definition will reveal a lot about your theology and your approach to evangelism.

- William Temple: "Evangelism is the winning of men to acknowledge Christ as their Saviour and King, so that they may give themselves to his service in the fellowship of his church."
- John Stott: "Evangelism means announcing or proclaiming the good news of Jesus."
- C. E. Autrey: "Evangelism is to bear witness to the Gospel with soul aflame and to teach and preach with the express purpose of making disciples of those who hear."
- Delos Miles: "Evangelism is being, doing, and telling the gospel of the kingdom of God, in order that by the power of the Holy Spirit persons and structures may be converted to the Lordship of Christ."
- Peter Wagner: "Evangelism is seeking and finding the lost, effectively presenting the gospel to them and persuading them

to become Christ's disciples, responsible members of his church."

- Lausanne Covenant: "Evangelism itself is the proclamation of the historical, biblical Christ, with a view to persuading people to come to him personally and so be reconciled to God."

- John Mark Terry: "Evangelism is presenting Jesus Christ in the power of the Holy Spirit so that people will become his disciples."

I like my own definition because it is short (less to memorize) and because it emphasizes the person to be proclaimed (Jesus Christ), the empowerer of the proclamation (the Holy Spirit), and the purpose of the proclamation (to make disciples). When you write your own definition, perhaps you can improve on what these writers have done.

To conclude this section, it may be helpful to explain the difference between *evangelism* and *missions*. Both evangelism and missions are concerned with helping non-Christians become Christians. They both involve preaching and personal witnessing. So what is the difference? The activity may be much the same, but the situation is different. Missions involves crossing geographical, cultural, or language barriers to communicate the gospel, while evangelism is witnessing within one's own culture. All true missions work involves evangelism, but not all evangelism is missions. Every Christian is called to be a witness, but not all Christians are called by God to be missionaries.

WHAT IS THE GOSPEL?

If biblical evangelism is "gospelizing," the evangelist surely needs to understand the gospel. The Greek word translated "gospel" is *euaggelion*. This word means "good news." The English word *gospel* means "God spell" or "God's story." Normally, we think of the gospel as the basic message of salvation.

Jesus explained the essence of the gospel to his disciples before he ascended into heaven. "He told them, 'This is what is written: The Christ will suffer and rise from the dead on the third day, and repentance and forgiveness of sins will be preached in his name to all nations, beginning at Jerusalem'" (Luke 24:46–47). This is the message the apostles preached: the death, burial, and resurrection of Jesus and salvation through belief in him.

If you study the sermons recorded in the Book of Acts, you will find the basic elements of the gospel mentioned by Jesus. In 1936, C. H. Dodd, a British scholar, published his now-famous book, *The Apostolic Preaching and Its Development.* Dodd believed that all the apostles preached the same gospel message, which Dodd called the *kerygma* ("proclamation" in Greek). Dodd wrote that the kerygma contained these elements:

- An account of the life of Jesus including his death, burial, resurrection, and ascension;
- An explanation of how Jesus fulfilled Old Testament prophecies;
- A theological presentation of Jesus as both Lord and Messiah (the Christ);
- A call to repentance and forgiveness from sin.

In recent years a number of scholars, most notably Michael Green, have disagreed with Dodd. They believe that the idea of a fixed kerygma is an oversimplification. The common view today is that the apostles simply announced Christ's arrival and they adapted their evangelistic approach according to the context of their audience. This does not mean that they changed or compromised the message. Rather, they varied their approach according to the situation, much as a pastor would speak differently to a children's class than to a senior adult group.

This varied approach is evident in the preaching of Paul. When he preached to the Greek philosophers on Mars Hill (Acts 17:22–34), Paul had an opportunity to preach to the intelligentsia of Athens and began by referring to a local religious shrine. By contrast, when Paul preached in the Jewish synagogue in Antioch of Pisidia, he began by referring to the Old Testament. Though Paul tailored his message according to the audience he faced, he always mentioned certain things. Paul presented the gospel in one verse in 2 Corinthians 5:19; in 1 Corinthians 15:3–5, he wrote an entire paragraph to achieve the same purpose.

However you present the gospel, it is essential to proclaim the death, burial, and resurrection of Christ (Rom. 10:9–10). Finally, you must remember that when you evangelize, you do not just encourage people to believe certain facts about Jesus; rather, you encourage them to establish a personal relationship with Jesus himself. Or, as one preacher declared, you need heart knowledge as well as head knowledge.

FIVE REASONS TO EVANGELIZE

Five basic reasons should motivate the church to reach out to a lost and spiritually dying world.

Reason #1: Evangelize to Follow Christ's Example

After his resurrection Jesus appeared to his disciples and said, "Peace be with you! As the Father has sent me, I am sending you" (John 20:21). That is, he was sending the disciples to complete the task he had begun. Jesus wanted the disciples to imitate his example. One reason why Jesus spent so much time with his disciples was because he wanted them to observe and imitate his actions.

Why did Jesus come to earth? He answered this question at Zacchaeus' house when he said, "For the Son of Man came to seek and to save what was lost" (Luke 19:10).

Jesus provided a marvelous example throughout his ministry. He modeled evangelism for his disciples, just as effective church leaders do today. Jesus' evangelism was personal, pointed, perennial, persuasive, patterned, powerful, and prayerful.

Personal. Jesus dealt with people personally. Leighton Ford has identified thirty–five personal interviews recorded in the gospels. Though Jesus often preached to crowds, he still had time to speak to individuals like Zacchaeus, Nicodemus, and the woman at the well. Jesus' evangelism was personal because he dealt with individuals in different ways. He varied his approach according to the person's understanding and needs. Jesus' conversation with Nicodemus (John 3) differed from his conversation with the woman at the well (John 4).[2]

Pointed. Jesus called people to a life of sacrificial discipleship. He offered them a cross to bear and a cup to drink (Mark 8:34–38; 10:38–39). Jesus challenged the rich young ruler to give up his wealth, and he challenged James and John to give up their fishing nets. Jesus required his disciples to fully commit their lives to him and his kingdom.

Perennial. Jesus evangelized people at all times and in all places. He spoke with the Samaritan woman at noon and Nicodemus at night. Jesus encountered Bartimaeus on a road and Zacchaeus in a tree. Jesus met Peter at the seashore and the thief on the cross. Even in his dying breath, Jesus led someone into the kingdom of God.

Pervasive. Jesus evangelized people from every race and social class. Although Jesus began his ministry among the Jews, he also ministered to Samaritans, like the woman at the well, and to Gentiles, like the Roman centurion. Jesus commanded his followers to make disciples of "all nations" (Matt. 28:19). This phrase could be translated "all ethnic groups." In this verse Jesus showed his concern for people of all races. Furthermore, he cared for the poor and outcast. Jesus healed the lepers and dined with tax collectors. He loved those whom most people despised. Jesus not only preached grace; he demonstrated grace in his ministry.

Patterned. Jesus modeled evangelism for his disciples. He told them what to do, demonstrated it, and sent them out to practice what he taught them by word and example. He used methods that were reproducible. Jesus set the pace and commanded His disciples to follow His example.

Powerful. The Holy Spirit empowered the ministry of Jesus. Mary conceived Jesus by the power of the Holy Spirit (Luke 1:35). Luke testified that Jesus was "full of the Holy Spirit" and "led by the Spirit" (Luke 4:1). Jesus sacrificed himself on the cross and rose from the grave by the power of the Holy Spirit (Heb. 9:14; Rom. 8:11). The power of the Holy Spirit permeated Jesus' earthly ministry and set an example for his followers.

Prayerful. Jesus' life demonstrated the importance of prayer. He awoke early in order to give himself to prayer. Jesus prayed at his baptism (Luke 3:21), when he chose his disciples (Luke 6:12), before he fed the five thousand, before he raised Lazarus (John 11:41–42), and in the garden of Gethsemane (Luke 22:39–44). Truly, Jesus depended on prayer to sustain his ministry. If Jesus found prayer indispensable, should modern evangelists find it otherwise?

Reason #2: Evangelize to Obey the Lord's Command

Jesus commanded his disciples to evangelize the world. This command alone should motivate Christians to evangelize faithfully. Mark 1 tells how Jesus called his first disciples. As Jesus walked along the Sea of Galilee, he saw Simon Peter and Andrew fishing and challenged them with these words: "Come follow me, . . . and I will make you fishers of men" (Mark 1:17). Simon and Andrew made their living catching fish and bringing them to the market. Jesus called them to the task of catching persons and bringing them into the kingdom of God. Notice their reaction: they left their nets "at once" and followed Jesus. Jesus calls all his disciples to the task of evangelism, the highest calling.

The commands of Matthew 28:18–20. In the Great Commission, Jesus explained what he wanted his followers to do. He also explained their authority, their assignment, and their assurance.

In verse 18, Jesus declared that he had received "all *authority.*" By his resurrection Jesus demonstrated both his messiahship and sonship. On the basis of who he was, Jesus possessed the authority to order his followers to evangelize the whole world. Therefore, Christians who evangelize do so in and through the full authority of Jesus Christ, the King of kings. One day Dwight L. Moody witnessed to a man on a Chicago street corner. The man took offense and said, "Why don't you mind your own business!" Moody replied, "This is my business."

In verse 19, Jesus commanded the disciples to "make disciples of all nations." This was their *assignment.* Notice, the command here is to make "disciples," not "converts." A disciple is a mature, reproducing follower of Christ. A convert is a new believer who is still a spiritual baby. Jesus desired followers who would "obey everything" he had commanded them to do. He desired a full, mature commitment, not just initial enthusiasm. Jesus instructed his followers to disciple all the peoples of the world. The word translated "nations" in verse 19 is the Greek word *ethne,* from which we get the English word "ethnic." The church's assignment, then, is to make more and more disciples in every ethnic group in the world until the whole world is discipled. That is certainly an intimidating task!

You may wonder why I have not yet mentioned the word "go" from this passage in Matthew. It is because the emphasis in the Greek New Testament is on the phrase "make disciples." Making disciples should be our primary concern and we will accomplish that by going, baptizing, and teaching.

In addition, Jesus spoke of the disciples' *assurance.* If modern Christians, with all their resources, find the Great Commission a daunting challenge, imagine how the eleven apostles must have felt. Ever sensitive, Jesus immediately gave them this assurance: "Surely I am with you always." Verse 20 reminds us that we do not work alone. Jesus Christ will be with us as we evangelize the world. Instead of feeling intimidated, we can declare the gospel with confidence, secure in the assurance of Jesus' divine authority and constant companionship.

The commands of John 20:21. Jesus explained the mission of the church in these words: "Again Jesus said, 'Peace be with you! As the Father has sent me, I am sending you'" (John 20:21). This verse helps us understand Jesus' vision for the ministry of his disciples. He wanted them to complete the mission he had begun.

Why did Jesus spend so much time training the disciples? Because he wanted them to carry on when he returned to heaven. Jesus knew his earthly ministry would last only a short time, so he prepared his disciples to carry on his work. You could say that he multiplied himself through his disciples. A veteran missionary once told me, "It is better to train ten people to do the work, than to do the work of ten people." Jesus modeled that proverb in his own life.

This verse also explains the nature of the church's ministry. Jesus not only challenged his disciples to carry on his work; he also directed them to do his work as he did it.

This direction implies at least three things:

1. Jesus commands us to *submit.* The basis of servanthood is obedience. Jesus himself prayed in the garden of Gethsemane, "Not my will, but yours be done" (Luke 22:42). In Romans 1:1 Paul described himself as a "servant" of Jesus Christ. Christian evangelists must submit themselves to God's authority.

2. Jesus commands us to *serve.* By his perfect example, Jesus modeled servanthood for us. In Mark 10:45 Jesus declared, "For even the Son of Man did not come to be served, but to serve, and to give his life as a ransom for many." Jesus served the people in almost every way imaginable by healing, feeding, comforting, and teaching them.

   Many people approach the church with a consumer's attitude: What can you do for me? Here is a better approach: What opportunities for service do you provide? Some church signs read: "Come help us grow!" Here is a more appropriate question for a church sign: "How Can We Serve You?"

3. Jesus commands us to *sacrifice.* He modeled sacrifice for his disciples by giving his time and energy for the people; ultimately, he sacrificed himself for humanity: " Now he has appeared once for all at the end of the ages to do away with sin by the sacrifice of himself" (Heb. 9:26b). By his words and actions Jesus demonstrated a sacrificial love for humanity. Likewise, pastors and church members must sacrifice time, money, and effort in order to reach people for Christ. Jesus has sent us to sacrifice just as He did.

The commands of Acts 1:8. Just before his ascension Jesus told his disciples: "But you will receive power when the Holy Spirit comes on you; and you will be my witnesses in Jerusalem, and in all Judea and Samaria, and to the ends of the earth." This statement is a blueprint for church evangelism. If you study Jesus' words carefully, you will discover three key elements:

1. The power of the Holy Spirit is essential for evangelism. Jesus mentioned empowerment before he talked about witnessing. Effective evangelists depend upon the Holy Spirit to convict people of their sin and convince them of their need for the Savior.

2. Jesus commanded his disciples to be witnesses. The Greek word used here, *martures,* refers to a group of people who testify to what they have seen and heard. The Greeks used this word to describe someone who testifies at a trial. Jesus instructed his followers to tell others what they knew about him. The memorization of Bible verses and evangelistic presentations are fine and good, but witnessing in its basic form is to simply tell what you know about Jesus. Every Christian is not called to be a "full-time" evangelist, but every believer should be a witness to the saving power of Jesus.

3. Jesus told the disciples where he wanted them to witness. They were to begin where they were, in Jerusalem; then they were to carry the good news to Judea and Samaria; finally, he directed them to carry the gospel to the whole world. These words of Jesus clearly teach us that missions is a natural outgrowth of local evangelism. Churches should maintain a healthy balance between local evangelism, home missions, and foreign missions. All three need our support and atten-

tion. Some churches effectively evangelize their local communities, but they seem to care little for the lost overseas. Other churches give large sums for foreign missions, but they do not evangelize their own communities. The same impulse that prompts the one should prompt the other.

Reason #3: Evangelize to Meet the World's Need

A sound theology of evangelism rests on the belief that people without Christ are lost and without hope of eternal life. Professor Roy Fish of Southwestern Baptist Seminary has stated that most Christians are functional universalists. A universalist believes that all people will ultimately be saved. Most believers reject that concept, but they live as if they believe it because they never witness to others. Most believers can quote John 3:16, but many forget that John 3:18 says, "Whoever does not believe stands condemned already because he has not believed in the name of God's one and only Son." Hell is not a popular topic in North American pulpits today. Still, we cannot escape its existence; ignoring it will not make it go away. Jesus often spoke of hell, and he warned people of the danger of going there. Pastors and churches must warn people of their precarious position. In Rev. 20:15, John wrote about the judgment of all people: "If anyone's name was not found written in the book of life, he was thrown into the lake of fire."

Jesus wept over Jerusalem because the people would not accept him (Matt. 23:37). Evangelistic churches today weep over their lost cities. Like Jesus, they are concerned that the people in their community are "harassed and helpless, like sheep without a shepherd" (Matt. 9:36). The physical, emotional, and spiritual needs of humanity move them to witness and minister to people in the name of Jesus.

Reason #4: Evangelize to Imitate the Early Church

Engineers planning to manufacture a new car begin by building a sample vehicle or prototype. If the prototype tests out well, they proceed with production. In a sense, the apostolic church at Jerusalem is our prototype. We should study the actions of this, the earliest Christian church, and imitate them. What did the members of the Jerusalem church do? After Jesus ascended into heaven, the disciples, obeying the command of Jesus (Acts 1:8), returned to Jerusalem and prayed for ten days (Acts 1:14). On the day of Pentecost, the Holy Spirit filled the apostles, and they proclaimed the gospel boldly (Acts 2:4). As a result of their preaching, they baptized three thousand people that day (Acts 2:41).

On another occasion the apostles prayed: they were filled with the Holy Spirit, and they witnessed boldly. Notice the progression here: *prayer–power–proclamation.* Their experience provides churches today with a good model to imitate. Students often ask me why we do not experience the events of Acts today. Surely, one reason is that we do not imitate their example. If we prayed until we were filled by the Holy Spirit, we, too, would see remarkable things today.

The early church also faithfully carried out Jesus' instructions in Acts 1:8 to preach the gospel in Jerusalem, then in Judea, and ultimately to the whole world. The Book of Acts explains how the church fulfilled this command. Peter took the gospel to Judea, Philip preached in Samaria, and Paul preached throughout the Roman Empire. Ancient church tradition holds that Thomas went all the way to India to preach the gospel. Many churches today call themselves "New Testament" churches. Churches that truly merit that description will devote themselves to evangelizing their community, their nation, and the whole world.

Reason #5: We Evangelize Because of Inner Compulsion

As mentioned above, the early Christians experienced the filling of the Holy Spirit, and they could not restrain themselves. They *had* to share the good news. Like a young woman with an engagement ring, they could not be silent. When the Sanhedrin commanded Peter and John to stop preaching, they declared, "We cannot help speaking about what we have seen and heard" (Acts 4:20). They were so excited about Jesus, they just could not keep quiet.

Christians also witness because the love of Christ moves them. As Paul wrote, "For Christ's love compels us, because we are convinced that one died for all, and therefore all died" (2 Cor. 5:14). The love and gratitude that Christians feel toward Christ moves them to share the good news about Jesus with all kinds of people (Rom. 1:14–15). The love of Christ living in believers' hearts moves them to have compassion on those who are lost and doomed to hell. True New Testament Christians love Jesus, and that love motivates them to witness and minister in his name.

SUMMARY

This chapter has explained the biblical mandate for evangelism; that is, gospelizing, sharing the gospel with people who are alienated from God by their sin. The gospel itself is the death, burial, and resurrection of Jesus Christ and the forgiveness from sin through faith in him. The church today has the responsibility to evangelize because of Christ's example, Christ's commands, the world's need to hear, the example of the early church, and the motivating love of Jesus Christ. Effective evangelism does not depend on the latest method or program. The early Christians did not have any materials or programs or seminars. They did have a deep conviction that Jesus was the promised Savior, an earthshaking power from the Spirit's filling, an all-consuming love for Christ, and devoted obedience to Christ's commands. It is no wonder they turned the world upside down.

STUDY QUESTIONS

1. Write your personal definition of evangelism.

2. What is the gospel? What elements are essential to a presentation of the gospel?

3. What are the characteristics of Jesus' evangelism?

4. What is the aim of evangelism according to Matthew 28:19?

5. What are three truths about evangelism taught by Acts 1:8?

FOR FURTHER STUDY

Coleman, Robert. *The Master Plan of Evangelism.* Old Tappan, N. J.: Fleming H. Revell Co., 1963.

Drummond, Lewis A. *The Word of the Cross.* Nashville: Broadman Press, 1992.

Green, Michael. *Evangelism in the Early Church.* Grand Rapids: Eerdmans Publishing Co., 1970.

Hobbs, Herschel H. *New Testament Evangelism.* Nashville: Convention Press, 1960.

Miles, Delos. "The Lordship of Christ: Implications for Evangelism." *Southwestern Journal of Theology* (Spring 1991): 43–49.

Miles, Delos. *Master Principles of Evangelism.* Nashville: Broadman Press, 1982.

Terry, John Mark. *Evangelism: A Concise History.* Nashville: Broadman & Holman, 1994.

CHAPTER 2

LEAD THE CHURCH TO PRAY

≫ ———————— ≪

Evangelistic churches emphasize prayer, especially prayer for the lost. In recent years, church growth experts like Charles Chaney and Peter Wagner have stressed the necessity of prayer in evangelism and church growth. Correct methods are important, but they are no substitute for prayer. The power of the Holy Spirit must animate the principles and methods. Kirk Hadaway writes, "Growing congregations are not only evangelistic and outreach oriented. They also place a greater emphasis on prayer."[1]

Thom Rainer says that a dynamic church must first become "a house of prayer," and he devotes a whole chapter in his book, *Giant Awakenings,* to congregational prayer.[2] Ken Hemphill writes that "the fuel for all growth is powerful prayer."[3] Hemphill is not speaking of typical church prayers: "We spend more time praying to keep dying saints who are prepared to die out of heaven than we do to keep sinners out of hell. There is little passion to our praying and little confidence that it really does matter."[4]

PRAY FOR POWER

If the Holy Spirit left your church today, would anyone notice? Does anything happen in your congregation that is not clearly due to human effort? Too few Christians and too few Christian churches are characterized by the anointing of the Holy Spirit.

Many church members are like those whom Paul described as "having a form of godliness but denying its power" (2 Tim. 3:5). If they do not deny the power of the Holy Spirit with their lips, they deny it with their lives.

We have the best in materials, media, and methods, but we lack spiritual power. Christians of the apostolic era had none of our advantages; they didn't even have the New Testament. Still, they turned the Roman Empire upside down. What impact does your church have in your community?

We cannot evangelize without God's power. I was reminded of this one day when I entered a classroom building. Mark, one of my students, was trying to wax the hallway floor, but the buffing machine wouldn't work. He said, "Doc, would you hold the plug in the outlet; I can't seem to get any power." When I held the plug in the electrical outlet, the buffer began to work. When I came to the class the next morning, that floor was shining! Now, Mark had equipment, training, and opportunity, but he lacked power. Once he got some power, good things began to happen. The same holds true for our churches; we have everything but the power of God. If we experienced and evidenced the power of God, good things would happen!

The first two chapters of Acts provide us with a case study of prayer and empowerment. In Acts 1:4–5 Jesus told his disciples: "Do not leave Jerusalem, but wait for the gift my Father promised, which you have heard me speak about. For John baptized with water, but in a few days you will be baptized with the Holy Spirit." Then he commanded them: "But you will receive power when the Holy Spirit comes on you; and you will be my witnesses" (v. 8). Notice that empowerment comes before witness.

The disciples did as Jesus instructed them. Jesus told them to wait in Jerusalem for empowerment. Acts 1:14 records their obedience: "They all joined together constantly in prayer, along with the women and Mary the mother of Jesus, and his brothers." The disciples prayed in the upper room for ten days, waiting for the Holy Spirit's anointing. According to Acts 2:2, when the day of Pentecost arrived, the disciples "were all together in one place." What were they doing? They were praying together, just as they had for the past ten days.

What did the disciples pray for? R. A. Pegram, a veteran Methodist pastor, answers the question:

> At Pentecost, I believe the disciples were praying not only for themselves, but also for the people of Jerusalem who had rejected Jesus. Many of those who had rejected Jesus were relatives, friends, acquaintances, and business associates. The disciples were interceding for Jerusalem with a oneness purpose. They wanted to see people come to believe in their resurrected Lord. When the Holy Spirit fell on those who were praying, I believe they were so filled with God's love that their prayers were set on fire for the people they knew.[5]

The disciples prayed for both power and results, and God answered both their requests. The Holy Spirit came on the apostles like a rushing wind, and they bravely stood and boldly declared the gospel. What a remarkable transformation! Fifty days before, these same men had cowered in locked rooms because they were afraid. Now they stood and proclaimed the gospel to the same people who had frightened them before.

Not only were the apostles empowered; their prayer for lost souls was answered. When Peter finished preaching, he gave an invitation and three thousand people responded. Notice that the wonderful response followed ten days of intense prayer and empowerment by the Holy Spirit. This is no magic formula, but the implications are clear. If we spent more time in prayer, we would have more power in our evangelistic efforts.

One might think that the church in Jerusalem stopped evangelizing in order to nurture the three thousand people just baptized. Not so. Acts 2:42 tells us that the Christians continued to devote themselves to prayer. What were the results of this fervent prayer? According to verses 43–47, the apostles performed miracles; the Christians were unified; they shared their possessions with the poor; they continued to worship daily; they met together in homes for fellowship; they won the favor of the people in Jerusalem, and they saw people come to believe in Christ every day.

If you compare the situation in the Jerusalem church with that of many modern churches, what comes to mind? Many of our churches today are divided into warring camps. Thousands of churches baptize no one in a given year. Most communities find the church irrelevant. What makes the difference? The power of the Holy Spirit. In order to fulfill the Great Commission, the church must access the power of the Holy Spirit through prayer. We need Spirit-empowered preaching, witnessing, and ministry. As Jesus said, "Apart from me you can do nothing" (John 15:5).

PRAY FOR GUIDANCE

Just before he ascended into heaven, Jesus told his disciples: "Stay in the city until you have been clothed with power from on high" (Luke 24:48). Why did Jesus say that? As you have just read, Jesus knew his disciples desperately needed the Spirit's empowerment. They would have gone into spiritual battle unarmed without it. Similarly, Jesus also knew that they needed guidance. How could they know where to go or what to do without the Spirit's guidance?

We might ask the same question of Jesus' modern disciples. How can we know where to go or what to do without guidance? There are almost unlimited needs and opportunities for ministry in every community—not to mention the overwhelming needs in the world. Obviously, a single congregation can't do everything. So, what do you do, and where should you do it? The Holy Spirit will answer those questions. If we pray for guidance and remain sensitive and alert to the Spirit's directions, the Spirit will direct us.

There are several examples of the Spirit's guidance in the Book of Acts. Acts 8 tells the story of Philip and the Ethiopian eunuch. An angel instructed Philip to leave his evangelistic meetings in Samaria and travel on the Gaza road. As Philip walked along, he encountered the Ethiopian eunuch. The eunuch was saved, baptized, and joyfully carried the good news of Jesus to Ethiopia. The angel's instructions must have seemed strange to Philip; after all, he was having tremendous results in Samaria. Nevertheless, he obeyed and met the eunuch. God providentially arranged the encounter. So, too, we must be sensitive to the Spirit, who will lead us to those who are ready to respond to the gospel.

Acts 9 recounts the conversion of Paul. After Paul was struck blind, he obeyed God and went to "Straight Street" to wait for help. God instructed Ananias to go to Paul's aid. Ananias could hardly believe his ears when God told him to go to Paul, but he obeyed, and Paul became the great missionary to the Gentiles.

In Acts 10 we read about Peter and Cornelius. God instructed Cornelius to send his servants to fetch Peter, and at the same time God used a dream to impress on Peter the Gentiles' need for salvation. "While Peter was still thinking about the vision, the Spirit said to him, 'Simon, three men are looking for you. So get up and go downstairs. Do not hesitate to go with them, for I have sent them'" (Acts 10:19–20). Peter did accompany them, and Cornelius was saved along with his household. I wonder how many divine appointments we miss today because we do not listen to the Spirit's guidance.

In Acts 16, Paul, Silas, Timothy, and Luke were traveling and ministering in Asia Minor. When they revisited the churches Paul planted on his first missionary journey, the missionaries tried to enter the province of Asia, where Ephesus was located. However, the Holy Spirit would not permit them to do so. Then they tried to enter the province of Bithynia, but "the Spirit of Jesus would not allow them to" (Acts 16:7). Finally, they went to Troas, apparently to wait for divine guidance. There Paul saw a vision of a Macedonian who begged him, "Come over to Macedonia and help us" (16:9). Paul understood immediately that this was God's will; therefore, he and his companions traveled to Philippi, where they founded an outstanding church.

These examples remind us that we can't work everywhere or do everything at once. We must rely on the Spirit's guidance to determine what we will do and when we will do it. Many churches are so busy doing good things that they neglect the best thing. Often the good is the enemy of the best. Doing good things may steal time, money, and effort from the best thing.

Through prayer we can discover what God wants us to do, where he wants us to do it, and when he wants us to do it.

PRAY FOR RESULTS

The first Christians prayed *powerfully*. Much of our contemporary prayer is either pointless or selfish. Many congregational prayers are so general they are meaningless. Most of our private prayers are wish lists of things we want God to give us or do for us. Acts 4:24–30 reports a remarkably different prayer offered by the members of the Jerusalem congregation. They prayed that God would enable them to preach with boldness and perform miraculous signs in the name of Jesus. What happened when they prayed this way? "After they prayed, the place where they were meeting was shaken. And they were all filled with the Holy Spirit and spoke the word of God boldly" (Acts 4:31). Notice the progression here: prayer, power, and finally proclamation. If we prayed as they prayed, we would be empowered as they were and we could preach as they preached.

The first Christians also prayed *specifically.* Acts 12 tells us how King Herod imprisoned Peter. The church feared that Herod meant to execute Peter as he had James, the brother of John. The believers prayed earnestly for Peter's release, and the night before Peter's trial, God sent an angel to release him. When Peter reached the street, he went directly to the house where the believers had gathered to pray. Ironically, the Christians were earnestly praying for Peter's release while he was in the street trying to get Rhoda to let him in.

The New Testament lists many objects for specific prayer. This list is not exhaustive, but it is illustrative. We are exhorted to pray for:

- Evangelists (Matt. 9:38)
- Missionaries (Acts 13:3)
- Rulers and authorities (1 Tim. 2:2)
- Open doors (Col. 4:3)
- New believers (Col. 1:9)
- Unity in the congregation (1 Tim. 2:8)
- The lost (Rom. 10:1).

We should pray specifically, and we should rejoice and thank God when he answers our prayers. Many Christians keep a prayer diary in which they record prayer requests and answers to prayer.

TEACH CHRISTIANS TO PRAY

Many Christians do not know how to pray. This fact became crystal clear to me a few years ago when I preached a sermon on prayer and suggested to the members of the congregation that they use the ACTS acronym as a guide for prayer.[6] We should pray with *adoration, confession, thanksgiving,* and *supplication.* I taught this formula to the congregation. After the service an elderly deacon approached me. He said, "I have been a deacon for thirty years and a Christian for forty, but no one ever taught me how to pray until now." That really disturbed me. How was it that he attended church all those years and no one taught him to pray? I'm sure he heard many prayers and exhortations to pray, but no one taught him *how* to do it. This should challenge us to teach our people to pray.

How do people learn to pray? By observation, instruction, and participation. Jesus' disciples saw him praying. Jesus often got up early in the morning and went to a solitary place in order to pray. We know that Jesus' example of prayer made a deep impression on the apostles, because they asked the church in Jerusalem to elect deacons so they would have more time to pray (Acts 6:4). Pastors and church leaders should model prayer for their people, not to be praised (Matt. 6:5–6), but in order to teach them. One's motive is the key factor here. We model prayer by praying and by the way we pray. When you pray, pray simply so that new believers can imitate you.

Believers also learn to pray by instruction. Jesus' disciples asked him, "Teach us to pray" (Luke 11:1). In response Jesus taught them the Lord's Prayer, or better, the "Model Prayer." You would do well to lead your people in a study of this prayer. The pastor should preach on prayer and lead a study group on prayer. The attendance may not be overwhelming, but it is better to disciple a few than none at all. Jesus spent most of his time teaching twelve men. If you only train two, you will still be better off than before. I highly recommend two resources for study groups on prayer: *MasterLife* and *PrayerLife*. Both of these will help your people learn to pray.

Adults learn best by doing, so lead your people to participate in prayer. It is not enough just to know about prayer; Christians must *pray*. Listed below are some ways to involve your members in prayer. Encourage them to participate and give them opportunities to share answers to prayer. This will inspire others to get involved. As you develop your prayer ministry, don't forget to enlist the senior members. They will shine in this ministry. They may not be able to fix the church roof or go on a mission trip, but they can pray.

DEVELOP A PRAYER MINISTRY

There are many ways to develop a prayer ministry. The important thing is to do it. In most churches prayer is an activity, but not an intentional ministry. We are seeking a fine balance here. Some things can be organized to death, so that nothing spontaneous happens. However, it is also true that everyone's business is no one's business. Organizing your prayer ministry will ensure that the church prays consistently and comprehensively. It will also pay dividends in evangelism. The First Baptist Church of Bonifay, Florida, developed an intercessory prayer ministry, and saw 118 additions, 56 baptisms, and an increase in attendance from 200 to 300 in just 8 months.[7] Here are some ways you can mobilize your members to pray.

Prayer Partners

Christians will pray more if they are held accountable. Encourage your members to enlist a prayer partner to pray with regularly.

Prayer Chains

Many churches have prayer chains. A prayer chain is a group of believers who have committed themselves to intercessory prayer. When a need arises, the members of the prayer chain pass the news and begin to pray for that situation.

Prayer Groups

Another popular approach is the prayer group. This is a group of Christians who meet together regularly for prayer and mutual encouragement. Today prayer groups are often called "small groups" or "cell groups." However, the idea is not new. The Pietists of the seventeenth and eighteenth centuries called them "cottage prayer meetings." Later, John Wesley organized groups and called them "classes." Whatever you call them, there is spiritual power in group prayer. You may also want to encourage your Sunday school classes to make prayer a significant part of the weekly meeting.

Whether you meet in small groups or Sunday school classes, if the members are committed to maintaining confidentiality they will feel free to share their deepest needs.

Special Days

Some churches are now designating special days for prayer and fasting (the purpose of fasting is to focus the mind on God). These may be in response to a special need or crisis. Whatever the prompting, devoting particular days to prayer and fasting is certainly biblical in nature. More churches need to do this, and when they do, I hope that they will pray for congregational and national revival.

Prayer Seminars

Many churches sponsor special seminars on prayer. For example, the First Baptist Church of Euless, Texas, held a seminar called "Praying the Heart of God."[8] An evangelistic meeting immediately followed, and more than three hundred persons made professions of faith. Pastor Claude Thomas said the seminar "was a vital part of the spiritual preparation."[9]

Prayer Rooms

Numerous churches have established prayer rooms or prayer chapels. These are rooms designated and equipped for prayer. The First Baptist Church of Sulphur Springs, Texas, did this. Every week forty members pray at least an hour for specific requests. The first year the prayer room was open, the volunteers prayed for twelve hundred requests. The church staff sends cards to those who have made requests informing them that someone prayed for them. Pastor David Hardage says, "We have seen a couple of full-fledged miracles, but some of the best things have been changes in the lives of those involved in the ministry—a newness and a freshness in their walk with the Lord."[10]

Prayer Retreats

Prayer retreats provide an opportunity for believers to learn more about prayer and to pray with fewer distractions. Prayer retreats are especially popular in Korea, where Christians often participate personally and congregationally.

Twenty-four Hour Prayer Ministries

Some churches have established prayer ministries that operate twenty-four hours a day. They see to it that a volunteer is praying at all times. Usually, this ministry is advertised, and the public is encouraged to submit prayer requests.

Prayer Hotlines

Another popular ministry today is the prayer hotline. In this ministry there is a designated telephone number answered by volunteers who pray with those who call. Again, this ministry is advertised as a church ministry. The requests may also be distributed to individuals or groups for further prayer.

Prayer Walkers

In a prayer walk, an individual Christian or group of believers walks through a neighborhood and prays for the neighborhood. This method was used by missionary Nan Sugg in Tainan, Taiwan, who tried traditional evangelistic methods. After a year, only one person responded. Then she did a prayer walk, going down street after street praying for the people, households, and businesses. She claimed Joshua's experience at Jericho as her inspiration. Soon after her walk people began to respond, and many Buddhists professed faith in Christ.[11] You may want to do a prayer walk in your community.

Prayer Request Cards

Many churches place prayer request cards in their pew racks. They encourage members and guests to make prayer requests. Other churches distribute attendance forms to all those attending worship. The forms include a space for writing prayer requests.

Staff Prayer

Most larger churches hold a weekly meeting for the church staff. Traditionally, these meetings emphasized planning and scheduling. Now, however, many church staffs are using this meeting to pray for the needs of their congregations and communities. They invite members to submit prayer requests, promising to mention these in prayer during staff meeting.

Prayer-grams

Prayer-grams are simply cards used to inform people that someone prayed for them. These may be sent out by the church staff or prayer ministry.

As you can see, there are many ways to conduct a prayer ministry. The main thing is to do something.

PRAYER AND SPIRITUAL RENEWAL

In his book, *An Endless Line of Splendor,* Professor Earle Cairns states that every great revival from the Great Awakening of 1726 to the present has begun with organized prayer groups. He says simply, "Prayer ranks first in the coming of revival."[12]

Dr. A. T. Pierson once said, "There has never been a spiritual awakening in any country or locality that did not begin in united prayer."[13]

A good example of prayer-inspired renewal is the Welsh Revival of 1904–1906. This revival was led by a young theology student named Evan Roberts. Roberts and some classmates attended an evangelistic meeting led by Seth Joshua. That night Joshua prayed, "O God, bend us." At the altar call Evan Roberts went forward and prayed, "O God, bend me." When he returned to campus, he felt a strong leading to return to his home church to preach. The college principal gave permission, and he returned home. Robert's pastor was somewhat skeptical of his request to preach, but he did allow him to address the prayer meeting, saying, "Our young brother, Evan Roberts, feels he has a message for you, if you care to wait."

Seventeen people remained to hear Roberts. He declared, "I have a message for you from God. You must confess any known sin to God and put any wrong done to man right. Second, you must put away any doubtful habit. Third, you must obey the Spirit promptly. Finally, you must confess your faith in Christ publicly." By 10:00 P.M. all seventeen had responded. The pastor invited Roberts to preach the next night and the next, and within two weeks a great revival was underway. Ultimately, one hundred thousand people were saved in the revival. Often, Roberts did not preach. He would stand and begin to pray aloud, and the Holy Spirit would move among the people in a powerful way.[14]

God will move in your church in a powerful way if you and your people will pray. Charles Haddon Spurgeon was one of the great pastor-evangelists of all time. Thousands of people were saved at his church, the famous Metropolitan Tabernacle in London. Once five college students went to London to hear Spurgeon preach. While they waited for the doors to open, a man approached them and asked, "Gentlemen, would you like to see the heating plant of this church?" The students weren't very interested in boilers, but they did not want to offend, so they agreed to go along. Their guide took them down a stairway and opened a door, whispering, "There is our heating apparatus." To their surprise the students saw seven hundred people bowed in prayer, asking God's blessing on the service about to begin. Gently closing the door, their guide introduced himself—Charles Haddon Spurgeon. With prayer support like that, it is no wonder that so many came to Christ at the Metropolitan Tabernacle.

A CASE STUDY

The Hebron Baptist Church in Dacula, Georgia, has grown from an average attendance of one hundred to over three thousand. What was the key factor to this church's growth? In an interview in the *Growing Churches* magazine, Pastor Larry Wynn made this statement:

> The turning point was the beginning of a prayer ministry. The foundation for this church growth movement has been a solid prayer ministry that began in the heart of a layman 18 years ago. I had become frustrated and discouraged early in my ministry. Things just weren't happening fast enough. I visited a layman I really didn't know very well and said to him, "James, I really don't know why I am here." He looked me in the eye and said, "I know why you are here. You are discouraged. The church isn't growing like you want to see it grow."
>
> I agreed and said, "This is a good church with good people and a lot of potential we have not realized."
>
> This layman's reply astonished me. "I know. I feel the same way," he said. "About six months ago, the Lord impressed on me the need to begin praying for this church. I began getting up about an hour earlier every morning to pray for you as the pastor, and to pray that God would give our church a vision.
>
> "About 30 days ago, I experienced peace in my heart and in my soul that God was going to give us a vision and that this was going to be a unique church. I really believe God wants us to reach Dacula for Christ." With only 1,800 people in the entire town at the time, that seemed like a reachable goal. Then James said, "I also believe God wants us to reach all of Northeast Georgia."
>
> "But how?" I asked.
>
> His response: "Prayer!"
>
> Then he said, "Why don't you invite a couple of guys over, and we'll meet on Thursday nights to pray for the church?"
>
> The prayer meetings were started. Nothing long. Nothing absolute. But what began to surface was that this little group of men began to capture a vision of what God could do in the church. Prayer was, and still is the cornerstone for church growth at Hebron Baptist Church.[15]

SUMMARY

Prayer is essential to church evangelism, as attested by both the Bible and church history. The first Christians at Jerusalem prayed until they were empowered by the Holy Spirit; then they evangelized their city in a mighty way. Christians should pray for power to carry out the Great Commission, and they should pray for guidance as they obey that divine command. When Christians pray, they should pray powerfully and specifically. An evangelistic pastor will teach church members to pray. A good way to pray is ACTS (adoration, confession, thanksgiving, and supplication). It is important to organize a prayer ministry. There are many ways to do this, but the important thing is to get believers praying consistently and systematically. Prayer is a key to renewal, and we will not experience revival in our time unless we pray.

STUDY QUESTIONS

1. On the day of Pentecost three thousand were saved. What did the believers do to prepare for that event?

2. What is one biblical example of God's guiding the church in evangelism?

3. What does the ACTS acronym represent?

4. What are three prayer ministries your church could and should implement?

5. What is the relationship of prayer to spiritual renewal?

FOR FURTHER STUDY

Bryant, David. *Concerts of Prayer.* Ventura, Calif.: Regal Books, 1988.

Christensen, Evelyn. *A Study Guide to Evangelism Praying.* Atlanta: Conger Printing, 1992.

Hemphill, Ken. *The Antioch Effect.* Nashville: Broadman & Holman, 1994.

Rainer, Thom S. *Giant Awakenings.* Nashville: Broadman & Holman, 1995.

CHAPTER 3

LEARN THE PRINCIPLES
OF CHURCH GROWTH

➤ ———————— ◄

Wise church leaders learn and employ the principles of church growth in order to win their communities to Christ. Some argue that we only need the power of the Holy Spirit to reach people. However, I believe that divine empowerment, hard work, and correct methods all combine to produce effective church evangelism. In the last chapter I mentioned Mark, the student who was trying to wax the floor. He surely needed power, but he also needed the proper materials and training to accomplish his task. A pious farmer will tell you that God provides the harvest; yet, the farmer also knows that he must work hard and use correct agricultural methods as well. In this chapter we will define "church growth" and teach you some of its basic principles.

WHAT IS CHURCH GROWTH?

Origin

Donald McGavran both coined the term *church growth* and developed the discipline known as church growth. McGavran served as a missionary for more than thirty years in India. He discovered that the churches in some districts grew, while in other districts they did not. He studied this phenomenon, and published his discoveries in a little book called *The Bridges of God* (1955). In 1959 he published *How Churches Grow,* and in 1970 he published his *magnum opus, Understanding Church Growth.* In all these books McGavran's primary concern was to help foreign missionaries plant and grow more churches.

As pastors in North America became aware of McGavran's ideas, they asked about applying McGavran's principles to local church situations. In the 1970s two of McGavran's disciples, Peter Wagner and Win Arn, began writing books and articles about how to grow churches in North America. Thus we can say that for the first twenty years, the church growth movement emphasized foreign missions; and for the last twenty years, it has concentrated on analyzing the whys and wherefores of local church growth. Foreign missionaries still study and use church growth principles, but even a cursory review of the literature reveals a marked shift toward local church growth methods.

Definition

Writers use the term "church growth" in a number of ways, but the official definition (if there is one) comes from the American Society for Church Growth:

> Church growth is that discipline which investigates the nature, expansion, planting, multiplication, function, and health of Christian churches as they relate to the effective implementation of God's commission to "make disciples of all peoples" (Matt. 28:18–20). Students of church growth strive to integrate the eternal theological principles of God's Word concerning the expansion of the church with the best insights of contemporary social and behavioral sciences employing as the initial framework of reference the foundational work done by Donald McGavran.[1]

This definition is a bit long and unwieldy. A shorter one is found in Peter Wagner's popular book, *Your Church Can Grow:* "Church growth means all that is involved in bringing men and women who do not have a personal relationship to Jesus Christ into fellowship with Him and into responsible church membership."[2]

Church Growth and Evangelism

What is the relationship between church growth and evangelism? My thesis in this book is that true church growth occurs when churches evangelize their communities. Apparently, Donald McGavran was thinking this same way in his last years. In 1988 he published a book entitled *Effective Evangelism,* and shortly before his death he told several friends and colleagues that he wished he had named his movement *effective evangelism.*

What was troubling McGavran? He knew, as do all informed observers, that many large, growing churches have grown primarily through transfer growth rather than conversion growth. Churches add members in three ways—through biological growth, transfer growth, and conversion growth. Biological growth refers to baptizing children of church members. Now it is surely important to lead young people to faith in Christ; but if you only win the children of your church members, then your church will plateau. Transfer growth occurs when people move their membership from one church to another. Certainly, people should transfer their church membership when they move from one city to another, but this is not *kingdom growth* (growth in the size of God's kingdom). Conversion growth happens when a lost person professes faith in Christ and is added to the membership of a local church. This is church growth that reflects growth in God's kingdom. Effective churches grow in all three ways, but the only way to truly fulfill the Great Commission is to emphasize conversion growth, which I will do in this book.

What, then, is the relationship between evangelism and church growth? It depends on how you define the two terms. Lewis Drummond, professor of evangelism at Beeson Divinity School, defines evangelism as "a concerted effort to confront the believer with the claims of Jesus Christ and to challenge him with the view of leading him into repentance toward God and faith in our Lord Jesus Christ and, thus into the fellowship of the church."[3] If we use Dr. Drummond's definition, we have a fine definition of conversion church growth, but there is no mention of transfer growth. This helps us to see that evangelism and church growth are closely related, siblings, in fact. However, church growth is broader than evangelism in that it also considers ways to reach and enlist unchurched or inactive Christians in the community.[4]

Church Health

In recent years several church growth writers have suggested that *church health* is a better term to use than church growth. Rick Warren, the innovative pastor of the Saddleback Community Church in Orange County, California, is one of these. He writes, "I believe the key issue for churches in the twenty-first century will be church health, not church growth. Focusing on growth alone misses the point. . . . Healthy churches don't need gimmicks to grow. They grow automatically. When our congregations are healthy, they will grow the way God intends."[5]

Warren believes that churches grow naturally, and a church that does not grow is unhealthy. Most church leaders attend church growth seminars hoping to answer this question: What will make our church grow? Warren says church leaders should ask a different question: What hinders our church from growing?

My son, Micah, is fifteen years old. He is a high-school football player and weighs over two hundred pounds. Now, I have not had to conduct a growth campaign for Micah. I don't have to encourage him to grow or send him to seminars on human growth and development. All I have to do is create the right conditions, and Micah grows naturally. His mother and I provide him with food (lots of it), rest, shelter, clothing, and medicine. His coach provides him with exercise. Clearly, we have created a good *growth climate* for Micah because he has really grown, and he shows no sign of stopping.

Most of the remainder of this book will concentrate on creating a climate for growth in your church. Warren and others make a good point about church health, and growth is certainly one characteristic of a healthy church. However, because *church growth* is still the more common term, that is the term I will use in this book.

WAYS OF CONSIDERING CHURCH GROWTH

Church growth writers have developed several different ways of considering church growth that help us understand the full nature of church growth.

Peter Wagner

Wagner has divided church growth into four categories: internal growth, expansion growth, extension growth, and bridging growth. *Internal growth* refers to spiritual and organizational growth. If the church members more fully develop their devotional lives, that would be internal growth. Three examples of internal growth are: the members of a church making an effort to more carefully develop their devotional lives, the establishment of a graded choir program, and the development of a recreational ministry program.

When he writes about *expansion growth,* Wagner refers to the numerical growth of an individual congregation. As I mentioned above, expansion growth can come through biological growth, transfer growth, and conversion growth.

Extension growth refers to church planting, that is, an existing church establishing a daughter church. The idea here is that the church extends itself by planting a new church or churches.

Bridging growth refers to cross-cultural evangelism and church planting. This type of church growth is essential to world missions. Wagner believes that a healthy church will grow in all four ways.[6]

Ebbie Smith

Smith is professor of missions at Southwestern Baptist Seminary. In his book, *Balanced Church Growth,* Smith states that God wants his church to grow bigger, better, and broader. By *bigger* he means numerical church growth. This would include both growth in the number of believers and in the number of churches. By *better* Smith means that the church members should grow more mature in their relationship with God and more ethical in their relations with other persons. By *broader* he means that the church should become more inclusive, incorporating persons from all the peoples of the world.

Rick Warren

Warren is the pastor of the Saddleback Community Church, a church that grew from two members to twelve thousand members in just sixteen years. Warren believes that healthy, permanent church growth must involve five dimensions. It must grow *warmer* through fellowship, *deeper* through discipleship, *stronger* through worship, *broader* through ministry, and *larger* through evangelism. All five dimensions are evident in Acts 2:42–47, and all five are necessary characteristics of a healthy church.[7]

Critics of the church growth movement have often complained that church growth proponents are only concerned about "nickels and noses," but the preceding material should show how unfair that complaint is. Wise pastors want their congregations to grow in every way.

THE 1•5•4 FORMULA FOR CHURCH GROWTH

Gene Mims, vice-president of the Church Growth Group at the Baptist Sunday School Board, has developed a helpful formula that helps us understand what a local church must do to achieve balanced church growth.[8]

The 1•5•4 Principle

1— Great Commission

5— Functions

- Evangelism
- Discipleship
- Ministry
- Fellowship
- Worship

4— Results

- Numerical Growth
- Spiritual Growth
- Ministries Expansion
- Missions Advance

One Great Commission

Mims believes that by following the "1•5•4 Formula" the church can cooperate with God in building his Kingdom. In Mims' formula, the number 1 represents the Great Commission. Like Rick Warren, Mims believes that the church's basic purpose is to fulfill the Great Commission (Matt. 28:18–20). Therefore, everything the church does should contribute to fulfilling the Great Commission in some way.

Mims believes the church must excel in fulfilling five functions in order to grow. He calls these five functions "the gateway to growth." They represent the five functions of the church taught in the New Testament.

Five Church Functions

Evangelism. Mims believes that evangelism is the key to true church growth. Rather than shuffling members from church to church, we must win people out of the world. God's plan for evangelizing the world is for Christians to share the gospel with the lost. Christians must "speak, live, and show His good news of salvation to persons separated from Him."[9]

Discipleship. The Great Commission challenges believers to "make disciples" of all the ethnic groups in the world. A disciple is a mature follower of Christ. Christian maturity requires personal holiness, ethical living, fervent witnessing, and congregational participation, characteristics that Jesus commanded of his disciples. The church must do everything in its power to help new believers become mature disciples.

Ministry. Mims defines ministry as "meeting another person's need in the name of Jesus."[10] Ministry involves helping people both inside and outside the church. By doing this, the church is simply following the example of Jesus and the early church. Though a person's spiritual needs are of ultimate importance (because they are eternal), there is no inherent conflict between ministry and evangelism. Ministry opens doors for evangelism, and evangelism brings us into contact with people who have physical and emotional needs. Christlike ministry is ministry to the whole person. All Christians receive a spiritual gift from the Holy Spirit to be used in ministry. When all believers exercise their gifts, needs are met; the church grows, and Christ is glorified.

Fellowship. Fellowship is more than coffee and cookies after worship. Fellowship involves the personal relationships church members develop with each other through the open-hearted sharing of life's joys and sorrows. People need to be part of a group. They need to be known by name and missed when they are absent. Mims writes: "People will not come where bickering, selfishness, coldness and tensions prevail. Who can blame them? People want to be where peace, joy, love, and family relationships prevail."[11]

Worship. Mims defines worship as "any activity in which believers experience God in a meaningful, spiritually transforming way. True worship should lead worshipers to a deeper appreciation for God, a better understanding of His ways, and to a deeper commitment to Him."[12] Worship is an essential function of the church, and failure in worship will lead to failure in other areas. Mims identifies eight elements of worship in the New Testament: prayer, praise, confession of sin, profession of faith, Scripture reading and study, preaching, ordinances, and giving. Mims acknowledges that these elements may be expressed in many different forms, but he insists that they are all necessary for true worship to take place.

Four Wonderful Results

Numerical growth. Some writers discount the importance of numbers and emphasize the importance of spiritual growth. As you've seen, both are important. In my experience, those who make the least of numbers are embarrassed about their growth statistics. The Book of Acts records several numerical reports. Why? Numbers represent what the church is doing. Each number, each statistic, represents a person won to Christ or baptized or enrolled in Bible study.

Numbers and statistics are important for tracing progress. Physicians insist on accurately monitoring their patients' vital signs. That monitoring is essential in discerning a patient's progress. The same holds true in a local church. Your church's statistics are its vital signs.

If a church diligently and effectively fulfills its five basic functions, then most likely the church will grow. I'm often asked if every church can grow. I always say "no." Some churches are in areas of declining population, and are not likely to grow. However, most churches can and should grow, at least to some extent. If we faithfully obey God's commands, then God will bless our efforts with numerical growth.

Spiritual growth. Mims maintains that another result of excellent fulfillment of the five functions is spiritual growth. In his view there are four characteristics of spiritual growth:

1. A developing relationship with Christ—becoming more like Christ.

2. A developing relationship with other believers—growing in love and unity with other Christians.

3. A developing relationship with the lost—developing friendships with the lost so that we can win them to Christ. Some call this "lifestyle evangelism," while others call it "friendship evangelism."

4. A developing use of Christian disciplines—growing through the practice of spiritual disciplines. These include prayer, Bible study, worship, witnessing, meditation, and fellowship. There are no shortcuts to Christian maturity.

Ministries expansion. New churches must first establish basic ministries such as worship and Bible study. Once those are in place, the church can begin to develop other ministries. These ministries should be determined by the spiritual gifts of the members and the needs of the community. A church cannot meet every need, but growing churches find themselves ministering in many more ways as God adds more gifted individuals to their congregations.

Missions advance. Growing churches pray for and practice missions. They are concerned not just about the lost in their locality; they are also burdened for those in other places who have never heard the gospel. In Romans 10 Paul asked a series of pointed questions: "How, then, can they call on the one they have not believed in? And how can they believe in the one of whom they have not heard? And how can they hear without someone preaching to them? And how can they preach unless they are sent?" (Rom. 10:14–15a). Obedient, growing churches know those questions and answer them. They send missionaries to reach all the peoples of the world. When churches get in touch with God, they find themselves cheerfully cooperating with his plan for world evangelization.

I like Mims's formula for several reasons. First, it is biblical; it emphasizes the Great Commission. Second, it is simple and easy to communicate. Third, it stresses the basic functions of the church. I agree with Mims that the key to balanced church growth is fulfilling Christ's commission and properly executing the basics. Athletic coaches often say, "If you execute the basics consistently, good things will happen." According to Mims the same is true in the church, and he's right.

PRINCIPLES OF CHURCH GROWTH

There are as many lists of church growth principles as there are writers. The following list summarizes principles gleaned from many different sources.

God Wants the Church to Grow

Church growth advocates believe that God wants all people to receive salvation through Christ and to be incorporated into the church. As more people accept Christ as their Savior, the church will grow. God wants the church to grow, not just for growth's sake but because those numbers represent people who are being saved.

Pastoral Leadership Is Essential

Church growth research consistently shows that the pastor's attitudes and actions are key factors in church growth. The people will not move beyond their pastor. A church will not necessarily grow because the pastor focuses on growth; but if the pastor is not concerned with growth, the church will not grow.

Churches Must Intend to Grow

A few churches grow without trying–usually because of their location. However, most churches must plan and work for growth.

Churches Must Set Goals

If you aim at nothing, you are sure to hit nothing. Growing churches prayerfully set measurable goals and work hard to achieve them. They should challenge and stretch the congregation, but not be so ambitious as to discourage the members.

Churches Must Research Their Communities

One of the great contributions of the church growth movement is the use of social sciences in the interest of missions and evangelism. Church leaders should employ anthropology and sociology to better understand their communities. The better you understand your community, the better you will know its needs. This knowledge will better equip you to develop ministries to meet those needs and reach people for Christ.

New Units Grow Faster Than Old Ones

Generally speaking, new churches, new Sunday school classes, and new small groups grow faster than old ones. Older churches, classes, and groups tend to bond together and exclude people outside the fellowship circle. This phenomenon is not inevitable or irreversible, but it is common. Thus, older churches can grow, but new churches tend to grow faster.

Church Planting Is Essential

New churches win more people to Christ than older churches. Research shows that new churches have a better membership-to-baptism ratio than older churches. New church starts is an important statistic in evaluating denominational vitality. Growing denominations start more new churches than the declining denominations.

Growing Churches Involve the Laity

Church growth emphasizes training and involving as many lay people as possible. Many writers focus on the importance of helping members discover and use their spiritual gifts for ministry and growth.

Growing Churches Keep Accurate Records

Growing churches carefully monitor their records to discern progress and problems. Church leaders should monitor these factors: baptisms, resident church membership, worship attendance, program enrollments, leadership training, volunteer involvement, stewardship, and mission support.

Methods Must Be Evaluated Regularly and Objectively

Church growth writers insist that church leaders must carefully evaluate the methods they use. It is easy to get into a rut and continue to use a method long after it has lost its effectiveness. Because time, personnel, and funds are limited, we must be careful to use all three in ways that are clearly beneficial.

Evangelism Must Be Culturally Relevant

Donald McGavran taught us to see the world as a cultural mosaic. Countries and communities are composed of different types of people. We must present the gospel to each group in ways that are linguistically and culturally appropriate.

Church Leaders Should Study Growing Churches

Much can be learned by studying growing churches. The leaders of these churches are typically imaginative and innovative. Some of their ideas may work for you; others may not. The mistake many young pastors make is that they try to clone successful programs. You may be able to clone methods, but you cannot clone a particular pastor's charisma or a specific community context. All methods must be adapted to local conditions.

OBSTACLES TO CHURCH GROWTH

Churches fail to grow for many reasons. Some of these factors are beyond control. Others, however, can be eliminated. Wise pastors ask, "What hinders my church from growing?" and they try to create a climate conducive to growth. The list below includes several reasons for lack of church growth. The items in the list are gleaned from several sources.

Many Churches Do Not Want to Grow

I used to think that all congregations wanted to grow. I've learned better. Many older congregations do not want to grow because they like things as they are. Growth would disrupt the status quo.

Many Churches Do Not Have a Conversionist Theology

These congregations do not believe that people need to profess Christ in order to be saved. They may believe that God will ultimately save everyone. If they believe that, there truly is no point in evangelism or missions.

Many Churches Have Lost Their Vision

Most new churches begin with a vision of growing and reaching their community for Christ, and they work hard to fulfill that vision for several years. However, after they have gained members and built their buildings, they lose their vision. In order to grow again, they must develop a new or renewed vision.[13]

Many Churches Do Not Match Up Sociologically with Their Local Communities

These churches decline because their communities change and they remain the same. For example, in Houston, Texas, many Anglo churches have declined because their neighborhoods have become Hispanic, but the churches have not provided Spanish classes or other services for them. If the people inside the church look and speak differently than the people in the neighborhood, the church must adjust or die.

Many Churches Decline Because of External Factors

Unforeseen events can hinder church growth. If a mine, factory, or military base closes, nearby churches will suffer. Sometimes an airport expansion or highway development will dislocate a church. The population shift from rural to urban areas has caused many rural churches to decline or die.

Many Churches Fail to Grow Because They Will Not Change

Many churches have not changed with the times, and unchurched people see them as irrelevant. The message of salvation never changes, but methods and programs must change with the times. Different generations have different cultures, just as different ethnic groups do. Chapter 4 discusses change at length.

Many Churches Fail to Grow Because of Poor Leadership

Many pastors are ignorant of church growth principles and methods. Others are knowledgeable but lazy. Church growth is hard work, and many pastors are simply not willing to make the effort.

Many Churches Fail to Grow Because Their Members Do Not Know How to Share Their Faith with Others

In these churches, very few members ever share the gospel with the lost.

Many Churches Fail to Grow Because Their Services and Programs Are of Poor Quality

I have attended churches and wondered why anyone would come back. In Sunday school the teacher simply read the quarterly to the class. In worship the announcements lasted fifteen minutes; the singing was listless, the service had no theme, and the sermon was boring. In such churches, the members attend in spite of the quality, not because of it. What would motivate a visitor to return?

Many Churches Fail to Grow Because of Internal Crises

Sadly, many churches are racked by dissension and strife. They cannot hope to grow until the conflicts are resolved.

Many Churches Fail to Grow Because
They Do Not Allocate Adequate Resources

Growing churches make outreach a priority in staffing, budgeting, and programming. Many churches say they want to grow, but they fail to provide the resources necessary to achieve growth.

Many Churches Fail to Grow Because
They Expect the Pastor to Do Everything

Many congregations look upon outreach as the pastor's responsibility. They see their role as paying and praying for the pastor.

This list may seem somewhat discouraging. Fortunately, not all churches suffer from the problems listed above, and many of these issues can be dealt with so that churches can turn around. When the hindrance is removed, the church can grow again.

More churches would grow if they knew the characteristics of growing churches.[14]

CHARACTERISTICS OF GROWING CHURCHES

It is possible to focus on methods but neglect or even forget the role of the Holy Spirit. We must avoid this temptation. The tower of Babel should remind us of what happens to people who try to build on their own wisdom and strength. In Matthew 16:18 Jesus said, "I will build my church." Furthermore, Paul wrote: "I planted the seed, Apollos watered it, but God made it grow" (1 Cor. 3:6). It is important to remember that truth.

While he served as director of the Southern Baptist Center for Church Growth, Ken Hemphill studied growing churches and discovered eight characteristics common to these churches being blessed by God with growth. A ninth characteristic is contributed by Rick Warren.

1. Growing churches have a profound awareness of the *supernatural empowering* of God to grow their church.

2. Growing churches have a serious commitment to *passionate prayer.*

3. The growing church experiences *Christ-exalting worship.*

4. Growing churches are led by *servant leaders.* Leadership is a function while servanthood is an attitude.

5. The healthy, growing church is marked by *kingdom family relationships*. Five relationships are important to a positive growth atmosphere: pastor to God, people to God, pastor to people, people to pastor, and people to people.

6. The growing church is possessed by a *God-sized vision*, a vision communicated by God to people who are obedient to the Great Commission.

7. The distinguishing characteristic of the growing church is a *passion for the lost*, a passion borne out of the theological understanding of the need of the lost and the mandate of the gospel.

8. Growing churches have a *commitment to discipleship*, the natural companion to the passion for reaching the lost. These churches develop members who can reproduce themselves in the lives of others.[15]

9. "Healthy, large churches are led by a pastor who has been there a long time. . . . A long pastorate does not guarantee a church will grow, but changing pastors every few years guarantees a church *won't* grow."[16]

SUMMARY

Church growth is the discipline that studies why and how churches grow. It is similar to evangelism but broader in scope because it also studies ways to enlist inactive and unchurched people. Church growth involves more than just numbers; it includes internal growth, extension growth, expansion growth, and bridging growth. A healthy church is a growing church, just as a healthy child is a growing child.

Churches should focus on fulfilling the Great Commission by emphasizing the five basic functions of the church: evangelism, discipleship, ministry, fellowship, and worship. Performing these five functions produces four good results: numerical growth, spiritual growth, ministries expansion, and missions advance. Churches must research, plan, and work in order to grow. Above all, they must depend on God to produce an abundant harvest of souls.

STUDY QUESTIONS

1. Who was the founder of the church growth movement?

2. What is Peter Wagner's definition of church growth?

3. In what three ways do churches add members?

4. What does Wagner mean by internal, expansion, extension, and bridging growth?

5. What is the 1-5-4 Formula?

6. Why is it important for a church to research its community?

FOR FURTHER STUDY

Hemphill, Ken. *The Antioch Effect: 8 Characteristics of Highly Effective Churches.* Nashville: Broadman & Holman, 1994.

Hunter, Kent R. *Foundations for Church Growth: Biblical Basics for the Local Church.* Corunna, Ind.: Church Growth Center, 1994.

Logan, Robert E. *Beyond Church Growth: Action Plans for Developing a Dynamic Church.* Old Tappan, N. J.: Fleming Revell Company, 1989.

Mims, Gene. *Kingdom Principles for Church Growth.* Nashville: Convention Press, 1994.

Rainer, Thom S. *The Book of Church Growth.* Nashville: Broadman Press, 1993.

Wagner, C. Peter. *Your Church Can Grow: Seven Vital Signs of a Healthy Church.* Ventura, Calif.: Regal Books, 1976.

CHAPTER 4

FACILITATE CHANGE IN THE CHURCH

W hen I was a boy growing up in Arkansas, the old folks used to say, "Two things in life are sure—death and taxes." Today we would have to add: "change." The world is changing at a rapid pace. The following prospectus of Vernon Armitage helps us understand the rate of change.

If human history was compressed into a fifty-year span, during the first forty-five years nothing much happened. Five years ago humans began to communicate by writing. Two years ago Christ came to earth. Five months ago Gutenberg invented the printing press. Twenty days ago Benjamin Franklin demonstrated that lightning is electricity. Nineteen days ago the telephone was invented. Eighteen days ago the Wright brothers flew an airplane for the first time. Ten days ago the radio became popular. Five days ago the people began to watch television.[1]

If you doubt the rate of change, try to run newly published software on your two-year-old computer. Where does this leave churches? Unfortunately, it leaves many of them far, far behind the change curve. Our North American culture is changing at a much faster pace than the churches can adapt to. Small wonder that many young people look upon the church as irrelevant. This chapter will help you understand the need for change and provide you with effective ways to help churches change.

45

TYPES OF CHANGES

Gordon McDonald, pastor of Grace Chapel in Lexington, Massachusetts, has listed a number of changes confronting churches today:

- *Economics.* Giving patterns and tax changes will make it difficult for churches to function in the future in the same way.

- *Technology.* Computer technology has made it possible for laypersons to acquire the same theological and biblical information as their pastor. Methods of communication are also changing so fast that the traditional church newsletter may soon be a quaint relic.

- *Relational realignment.* McDonald describes the nuclear family as "almost a nonexistent dinosaur in many parts of the country."

- *Generational segmentation.* Longer lifespans have led to a situation where five generations are alive at the same time. Each of these generations has a different learning and musical style.

- *1990s version of spirituality.* Modern people are interested in spiritual matters, but spirituality today is do-it-yourself. Most younger people reject absolutes in religion in favor of relativism and pluralism.

- *Exhaustion.* Longer working days and weeks have brought many employees to the point of exhaustion. The fact that more and more mothers work outside the home means fewer volunteers for church programs and projects.

- *Population mobility.* As American society becomes increasingly mobile, churches will find their membership turning over more rapidly. McDonald notes that 60 percent of an urban congregation may move within a thirty-month period.

- *Consumerism.* American denominations were built on the loyalty of people to a particular denomination. Younger people today have little loyalty to a denomination. Instead, they shop around for a church that meets their particular needs.

- *Single-issue mentality.* People today are increasingly polarized over ethical and political issues. Doctrinal purity may take second place to ethical matters.

THE NEED FOR CHANGE

Many churches today are struggling with change issues. Win Arn, a noted church growth writer, suggests that churches are struggling with the transition from the old paradigm to the new paradigm. He defines a paradigm as a grid of values and rules through which we interpret and understand our lives. Paradigms determine how we think about things and how we do things.[2]

Most churches still operate according to a 1950s paradigm. The 1950s was a great decade for churches.[3] All denominations experienced tremendous growth, especially from 1950–1955. In part, the postwar baby boom contributed to the growth, but many denominations aggressively sought to grow by means of evangelism and church planting. For example, the Southern Baptist Convention conducted a Sunday school membership campaign in 1954 entitled, "A Million More in '54." Further, the members of the GI generation demonstrated tremendous loyalty to the churches and denominations in which they were raised.

In a sense, many churches are prisoners of their success. I have visited many churches and inquired about their growth history. When the records are pulled out, they show the churches experienced their highest levels of attendance in the 1950s. Typically, these churches have continued to use the same methods they used in the 1950s. After all, they worked fine then! Veteran church workers have often said, "If we would just return to the methods we used then, we could grow again." Are they correct? Should we go back to those tried-and true-methods?

Unfortunately, such appeals are unrealistic. The situation today is so different that many methods used in the fifties just won't work. My father's 1956 Ford was a good car then, but I wouldn't want to drive it today (except perhaps to a car show). I enjoy driving a car with cruise control and a stereo cassette player. Then, too, many churches are using 1950s methods but with little or no success. Win Arn estimates that 80–85 percent of the churches in the United States are plateaued or declining.[4] Whatever methods they are using just are not working.

Someone has said insanity is doing the same thing over and over but expecting the result to be different this time. For example, Bethany Church has always conducted Vacation Bible School during the daytime. Finding workers is increasingly difficult because many of the women of the church work outside the home. Nevertheless, the church continues to do the same thing in the same way out of habit and tradition.

The churches have to find ways to reach new generations. In fact, Leith Anderson has addressed this need in his helpful book, *Dying for Change.* Sadly, Anderson's title is all too apt. Thousands of churches die every year because they refused to change.

Several years ago, John Bisagno, pastor of the First Baptist Church of Houston, Texas, became concerned about the declining churches in the Houston area. When he researched the problem, he learned that 114 Southern Baptist churches were in danger of dying. Further research showed that most of these churches declined because the congregations had refused to adapt to their changing neighborhoods. Their communities changed, but the churches didn't. In many cases the neighborhoods had become Hispanic, while the churches continued to offer services in English.

Baptist churches aren't the only churches with this problem. A colleague told me about a church in Canada that was founded by German-speaking people. After many years of existence in Canada, the church still worships only in German. In fact, the church advertises in the local English-language newspaper: "All Services in German; Everybody Welcome!" The services in German may be a blessing and comfort to some older folks, but you have to wonder how much impact that church has in its community.

Demographers tell us that the percentage of ethnic people in the United States is growing and will continue to grow. By the year 2000, 36 percent of the U.S. population will be ethnic. Churches will have to change in order to deal with these ethno-linguistic realities.

The changes in our society are not just ethnic; many are generational. When I get in my car after my children have driven it, I always have to change the radio station. They listen to different music than I listen to. Churches that want to reach baby boomers (those born 1946–1964) and baby busters (those born 1965–1975) will have to change their worship styles and programming. Churches that refuse to change will see their congregations age and decline.

OBSTACLES TO CHANGE

Whenever I teach church evangelism, my students say, "Doc, we know what you're telling us is right; we just can't get our members to accept it." What they are telling me is that their members resist change. This response has prompted me to include units on change in my courses (and a chapter in this book). The best methods in all the world are of no value if you can't persuade your people to adopt them.

One important element of facilitating change is understanding the psychology of change. The better you understand the obstacles, the better you will be at devising strategies to overcome resistance.

People resist change for many reasons. Familiar things make us feel more secure. Many people, particularly the very young and very old, become disturbed when their routine is disrupted. I can understand that. I don't like it when my wife rearranges the furniture. I like everything to stay the same! Lots of people feel that way, and they won't thank you for making changes.

Many people, especially the elderly, are quite frustrated with the pace of change in modern society. When they call their banks, they get a computer instead of a person. When they call the electric company, the clerk wants to know their numbers, not their names. One aspect of their frustration is their lack of control over these changes. They can't control what the bank does. Of course, they could move their accounts, but that would also involve change. When it comes to church matters, however, people do have a voice and a vote. They may make a last stand against change in the church business meeting. Church leaders who seek to make changes must remember that much opposition to change may be a knee-jerk reaction to change in general.

People also resist change because they see it as a threat to tradition. Naturally, older churches are more prone to this than newer churches. Church traditions are not inherently good or bad. They may serve to unite the church, but they may also serve to slow the church's progress and decrease its effectiveness. For example, many rural churches have traditionally held fall and spring revivals. The purpose of these revivals is to win the lost, and at one time many made professions of faith during these meetings. However, in most of these churches that no longer happens. Only the members attend, and often only a few. Nevertheless, the churches continue to conduct the meetings because they have "always done it that way." Rather than attack traditions head on, wise church leaders seek to modify traditions in order to make them more effective.

Lay leaders may resist changes because they see them as threats to existing power structures. Be assured that every church has a power structure; there are certain people who govern the affairs of the church. These powerful individuals may not speak out in business meetings, but their opinions are crucial. They may see suggested changes as a means of shifting power to the pastor or other laypersons. Therefore, they will judge the changes not on their merits, but on the basis of power issues. One way to avoid this problem is to include these people in the planning and thus enlist their support for the changes. One thing is for sure—you will have to deal with them sooner or later!

Sometimes people oppose change because they interpret it as personal criticism. For example, if a new pastor wants to change the order of the service, the minister of music may interpret that as a criticism of what he has been doing. Or, if a change in the methods used by greeters and ushers is suggested, it may be interpreted as a criticism of the ushers and greeters. Here is a good principle to always remember: *Any suggestion of change has the potential to offend someone.*

Some congregations resist change because they are unconcerned about the lost. They care more about maintaining the status quo than outreach. Rick Warren writes: "Let's be honest. Churches that refuse to change programs, methods, styles of worship, buildings, or even locations in order to reach a lost world for Christ are being *unfaithful.* With unreserved commitment to our Lord and Savior we must be willing to say, 'We'll do whatever it takes to reach people for Christ even if that means learning a new style of ministry.'"[5]

Well, is change a hopeless case? No, not at all. You just have to take prevailing attitudes into account and prepare the people for the changes. For example, you might ask the ushers committee to view a set of videos on greeting and ushering techniques and develop their own plan. If this is part of a church-wide evaluation, they will not feel singled out.

Members may resist changes not because they are against change, but because they disagree about the nature of the proposed changes. Usually, some folks will agree that changes are needed, but they may disagree over what ought to be done. They often suggest that what is needed is a slight modification of what is currently being done—in other words, let's do the same things, only better.

Finally, many people resist change because they are operating on invalid assumptions. They believe that what was previously true continues to be true. They may also believe that the conditions that contributed to the church's growth in the 1950s still prevail. Folks who drive to church from miles away may not realize that most of the church's neighbors now speak Spanish. They may believe that the nuclear family made up of mother, father, and two children (ideally a boy and a girl) is still the most common family type (it isn't). Some of these people are in denial; they find it painful to face reality.

One way to help these people accept change is to do some careful research on the church and its community. Many times a graph or chart can serve as a wake-up call to a church. George Barna's book, *The Frog in the Kettle,* helps to drive home this point. Often the decline of a church and the deterioration of its relationship to the local community are so slow and so subtle that the church does not realize it is dying. Churches can engage in denial just as individuals can.

IMPLEMENTING CHANGES

The list of obstacles above might intimidate the bravest change agent. However, there is cause for hope. Though change is seldom easy, it is possible.

Most churches must change in order to reach their communities for Christ. Unfortunately, it's rare to find a church that says, "We know we've got to make some changes around here. Just tell us what we need to do." Nevertheless, given good leadership, it is possible for churches to change. What must you do to lead your church through the change process? A growing body of literature exists that can help you plan the change process and minimize the pain. The following paragraphs offer a synopsis of available literature:[6]

1. *The pastor should lead the church to agree on its mission.* This mission is the church's purpose for being and should be expressed clearly in a mission statement. Many older churches have lost their sense of mission, so this step is very important.

2. *The church should set goals to accomplish the church's mission.* The members of the congregation should set goals only after much prayer. These goals should be measurable or tangible. Otherwise, they won't know if they attain them. A goal might be to increase Sunday school enrollment by 50 percent in twelve months, to baptize twenty people in the next year, or to begin a visitation program. A good goal is both challenging and realistic. It should stretch the members' faith, but it should not be so lofty as to discourage effort. A goal can help a church lift its sights to new possibilities.

3. *The pastor should enlist key leaders in the change process.* It is essential to involve influential people in the planning. Enlisting the participation of these people will ensure their ownership of the plans that are made. Most church leaders don't like surprises, so bring them on board long before you make any public presentations. Notice the possessive pronouns they use. If they keep saying "your" plan, you've got trouble; but if they say "our" plan, you will likely succeed. These key leaders will influence others to support the changes.

4. *The leader must constantly direct the members' attention to the church's mission and goals.* If the members focus their attention solely on the changes, the changes will probably fail. Few are motivated to change for change's sake. Instead, the leader must help the people see how changes are essential to accomplishing the church's goals and fulfilling the church's mission.

5. *The leader can improve the climate for change by increasing discontent with the status quo.* This may involve preparing some charts and graphs that show the church's decline in membership and attendance. Often, a church declines so slowly that even lay leaders don't notice, and a graphic demonstration can sometimes serve as a wake-up call for church leaders.

6. *The leader can speed change by increasing the attractiveness of the proposed goal or goals.* This involves demonstrating the good results the church can expect. Success stories from the church's past or other churches will motivate members. One helpful method is to take key leaders to visit a church that made the changes you are urging. When they see the good results at the other church, they will join your team of change agents.

7. *The leader should discuss the changes often. Use every opportunity to speak or write about the plan.* This keeps the changes on the front burner by regularly reminding the people of what still needs to be accomplished.

8. *The leader can ensure successful changes by enlarging the group that supports change.* Wise legislators count their supporters before they bring a bill to a vote. Wise pastors do the same. A few more weeks of persuasion may prove beneficial. It is important not to rush the change process.

9. *The leader must be open and flexible.* Others may offer suggestions that will improve the plan. Also, circumstances may change, prompting changes in the plan. Sometimes half a loaf is better than none. You may find it expedient to compromise on details in order to save the project.

10. *Remember that change agents must achieve and maintain a high level of trust.* People will follow a leader they trust. Building trust takes time. This is especially true in rural churches. In smaller churches relationships are more important than ideas. Develop friendships with key leaders before you propose major changes.

PRESENTING PROPOSED CHANGES

How should changes be presented to the church? "Very carefully" is the trite but true answer. A good presentation may make all the difference between acceptance and rejection. As you prepare your presentation, remember these principles:

Principle #1: Be Thoroughly Prepared

Anticipate questions and objections. Expect people to ask: "How long will this take? How much will it cost? Who will do this?" If you can't answer these practical questions, your plan will seem "half-baked." Ask supportive members to respond to questions. In fact, if you can persuade a respected lay leader to present the proposal, you will be miles ahead.

Principle #2: Prepare Handouts, Audiovisuals, and Other Items

Present your ideas logically. Start with the church's mission statement. Discuss the goals that will fulfill the purpose. Explain the changes needed to accomplish the goals. Demonstrate that changes are merely a means to a desirable end.

Principle #3: Do Not Criticize What Has Been Done in the Past

Many of the people listening to you did those things in the past. So the presentation should focus on positives. Listen to the responses carefully and analyze what lies behind the words that are spoken.

Principle #4: Avoid Becoming Defensive

You don't want the members to interpret your call for change as personal criticism, so don't interpret their remarks as personal criticism. Focus on the issues. Many leaders view objection to and/or rejection of their ideas as personal rejection. Sometimes this is true, but often they are mistaken. More likely, such responses reflect a genuine desire to understand the proposal or a negative reaction to change in general.

Principle #5: Expect Opposition

If you expect opposition, you won't be disappointed. Expect it and deal with it. Give the people time to get used to the idea. Don't force a vote on the plan at its first hearing. People don't like to feel pressured.

FINAL WORDS OF CAUTION

Changing a church is difficult, no matter how many books or articles you read. Some churches will refuse to change no matter what. Their last words will be, "We never did it that way before." If you are convinced that changes are necessary, please keep the following truths in mind.

1. *The older a church is, the more difficult it will be to change.* In my experience, older churches resist changes more stubbornly than new ones. This may be true because they have more traditions or more elderly members. Whatever the reason, it is true. A young pastor visited me once to ask for advice about his church. He pastored a hundred-year-old rural church. He wanted to disband all the church's organizations (including Sunday school) and implement a program of small groups. I

advised him against trying this, but he insisted. You can imagine the results.

2. *The more rural a church is, the more difficult it will be to change.* Rural people deal with change less often than city folk and are generally less tolerant of it.

3. *Student pastors will find it especially difficult to make significant changes.* Church members look on student pastors as temporary leaders and know they will be gone in a year or two. They have seen student pastors come and go. Therefore, they are not motivated to embark on long-term projects with them. Few student pastors served the church long enough to develop a high trust level.

4. *Be careful when you return home from the church growth conference.* The success of others can truly be intoxicating, but you can't duplicate personalities or situations. Most rapidly growing churches are in communities that are conducive to church growth. Your community may have very different demographics. Also, I'm convinced that the pastor's charisma is a key factor. Pastors of some megachurches would experience growth using any method simply because of their powerful personalities and spiritual gifts. But few pastors are so gifted. Be careful to adapt methods to your personality and your situation before you propose them to your church.

5. *Don't believe the members of the pastor search committee when they say the church wants to implement changes.* Often, this desire for change reflects the feelings of the committee, not the church. Even if support for change may be widespread, it may not be deep. Many congregations know they need to change, but they balk when the changes invade their comfort zones. Assume that making changes in the church will be difficult. Following the steps outlined above won't guarantee success, but it will make success more likely.

SUMMARY

Most churches need to change in order to reach more people for Christ. Change is difficult for most people, and it is particularly difficult for churches. Older and rural churches will find it particularly difficult. Wise pastors will plan changes carefully and proceed slowly; they will spend the time necessary to enlist the support of key lay leaders. Furthermore, they acknowledge the pain of change, believing that reaching more people for Christ is worth the pain.

STUDY QUESTIONS

1. What types of churches are hardest to change?
2. What are three obstacles to change?
3. Why is it important to write a mission statement before implementing changes?
4. Why should the change agent solicit the support of key lay leaders in the church?

FOR FURTHER STUDY

Anderson, Leith. *Dying for Change.* Minneapolis: Bethany House, 1990.

Van Auken, Phil and Johnson, Sharon G. "How to Make Changes Smoothly." *The Baptist Program* (June/July 1988):7–8.

Rainer, Thom. *Eating the Elephant.* Nashville: Broadman & Holman, 1994.

Schaller, Lyle. *The Change Agent.* Nashville: Abingdon Press, 1972.

Schaller, Lyle. *Strategies for Change.* Nashville: Abingdon Press, 1993.

CHAPTER 5

PLAN FOR EVANGELISM

❯❯ ———————— ❮❮

Most churches hope to reach the lost, but they do not have a plan for doing so. They have vague hopes but no concrete plans. This lack of intentionality is reflected in church growth statistics. Eighty to 85 percent of Protestant congregations in the United States are plateaued or declining.[1] Many of these churches are *efficient,* but not *effective.* Peter Drucker, author of popular books on management, says, "Efficiency is doing things right. Effectiveness is doing the right things."

Many churches operate efficiently. Their services begin and end on time. They send out attractive newsletters, and they mail contribution statements promptly. The organist never plays a wrong note, and the ushers never fail to seat guests or take the offering. The young are married, and the old are buried, but few are saved. Most of these churches baptize a few children each year, but they are not reaching their communities for Christ. They sponsor activities, yet they are not productive. They have forgotten their basic purpose—to make disciples locally and globally. In this chapter you will learn how to plan for outreach and evangelism.

THE NEED FOR PLANNING

Planning Is Biblical

Occasionally I meet someone who does not believe in planning. These people claim that the Holy Spirit spontaneously leads them to do what he wants them to do. What about that mind-set? As you've already read, it is important to be sensitive and responsive to the Holy Spirit. Sometimes he does interrupt our schedules; however, the Holy Spirit can also guide our planning. A careful study of the Scriptures reveals that God himself made plans. Exodus 25–30 details God's plans for the tabernacle. Jeremiah 31 tells how God planned for a new covenant community. In the Garden of Gethsemane Jesus asked God to change his plan for the salvation of humanity. Finally, Acts 1:8 shows that Christ had a definite plan for world evangelization. The Book of Acts recounts how carefully the early church followed Christ's plan.

Planning Is Practical

You've probably heard the old saying, "To fail to plan is to plan to fail." As you've already learned, most churches reach only a few people for Christ. One reason for this is lack of planning. If we fail to plan for evangelism, we will fail to evangelize. Through careful planning we can ensure an appropriate emphasis on evangelism and an adequate allocation of resources for that purpose. Without planning, our efforts will be disjointed and uncoordinated. When I need to make a trip, I plan for it. I call for airline reservations, a rental car, and a hotel room. Or, if I'm driving, I check the road atlas to determine the best route and the time necessary for the journey. Advance planning helps me get where I want to go. If you want your church to reach people for Christ, you need to have a plan for getting there.

Planning Is Economical

By planning your church's evangelism program you can save time and money. Carpenters build a house according to a plan called a blueprint. Following the plan saves time and materials. It works the same with evangelism; a plan saves time and money.

ORGANIZE AN EVANGELISM COUNCIL

The first step in planning for evangelism is to appoint or elect an evangelism council. Some churches call this the evangelism committee. If your church does not have committees, you might want to call it the evangelism task force or task team. Whatever name you give it, this council will help plan and promote evangelism in your church.

Since the purpose of the council is to lead the church in evangelism, the council should be made up of members who are concerned about, believe in, and practice evangelism. A local church asked a seminary professor to be an advisor for its evangelism program. When he met with the evangelism committee, only the chairman actually believed in doing any kind of evangelism. It's no wonder that the church is experiencing a severe decline.

The pastor should guide the selection of council members. If they must be nominated by a nominating committee, the pastor should meet with the committee to ensure that concerned people are nominated. Preferably the council should number no more than five. The more people you have, the harder it is to get them together to meet.

The organizational structure of the council should include a chairman and four task force leaders. The pastor and other staff members should serve as *ex officio* members. The four task force leaders are:

1. *Prayer Leader.* This person organizes and leads the church to pray for the lost.

2. *Training Leader.* This person plans and implements evangelistic training events throughout the year.

3. *Special Events Coordinator.* This person leads in planning and conducting special evangelistic events, such as revivals or concerts.

4. *Witnessing Leader.* The witnessing leader helps to organize and promote personal witnessing throughout the year.

Many small churches do not have enough members to staff a council like this. In a smaller church the pastor and one concerned layperson will fulfill these functions.[2]

DEVELOP A MISSION STATEMENT

What is a mission statement? There is much material available today on vision, mission, and purpose statements. These terms are defined and used by different writers in different ways (surprise!) and are often used interchangeably. I will differentiate between a mission statement and a purpose statement. A mission statement is a broad statement that expresses two facts about your church in general terms: what your church is and your church's overarching objectives. A mission statement is more philosophical, while the purpose statement is more specific.

Here is the mission statement composed by the First Baptist Church of Owenton, Kentucky:

> The mission of First Baptist Church of Owenton is to be a loving, obedient, ministering Body of Christ which, under the guidance of the Holy Spirit: proclaims the good news of salvation through Jesus Christ; encourages the growth of Christian love through worship, teaching, training, and fellowship; expresses Christian love by ministering; and reaches out with other Christians to the whole world to the glory of God.

I believe that the mission statement should reflect the Great Commission found in Matthew 28:18–20. It may be incorporated explicitly or implicitly, but every church should make that commission central to its mission. When we stray from the Great Commission, we have departed from the church's reason for existence.

How can a church develop a mission statement? The pastor must take a leadership role in developing the church's mission statement in collaboration with an appropriate group of lay leaders. Depending on the church's form of organization, this group might be the church council, the board of elders, the evangelism council, or an ad hoc committee convened for this purpose. The group should review relevant biblical passages and other churches' statements. Then they should spend considerable time in prayer. The church deserves a statement that is biblical, functional, and divinely inspired.

STATE YOUR PURPOSE

What is a purpose statement? Burt Nanus, in his book *Visionary Leadership,* defines a purpose statement (often called a vision statement) as "a realistic, credible, attractive future for your organization."[3] George Barna, in *The Power of Vision,* defines a purpose statement as "a clear mental image of a preferable future imparted by God to His chosen servants and is based upon an accurate understanding of God, self and circumstances."[4] A purpose statement should express what your congregation expects your church to be and do in its local environment. Many churches might share your mission statement, but your purpose or vision statement should relate to your particular local situation.

The following examples of purpose/vision statements may help you to better understand their function. The purpose statement for Saddleback Community Church reads: "To bring people to Jesus and *membership* in his family, develop them in Christlike *maturity,* and equip them for their *ministry* in the church and life *mission* in the world, in order to *magnify* God's name."[5]

An evangelical church in New York adopted this statement: "To equip professionals in New York City to impact their web of relationships, focusing on reaching non-Christians through cell groups and marketplace ministries that address urban needs." A church in southern California stated that its purpose was "to present Christ in a contemporary, creative, credible and caring way to all people in an environment where people from the community can grow to their full potential in Christ."[6]

Why do you need a purpose/vision statement? First, a purpose statement will help keep your church on track. It determines both what your church will and won't do. Many churches forget the Great Commission and develop all kinds of peripheral activities. These activities may be wholesome and helpful, but they distract the church from its main purpose. Everything a church does should contribute to fulfilling the Great Commission. Most church members are not clear on this. Win Arn, a church growth researcher who surveyed one thousand churches, asked the question, "Why does the church exist?" Eight-nine percent of the church members answered: "The church's purpose is to take care of me and my family's needs." Only 11 percent answered, "The purpose of the church is to win the world to Jesus Christ." Arn also surveyed the pastors of these same churches. Ninety percent of the pastors said the purpose of the church was to win the world to Christ, and 10 percent said it was to care for the church members.[7]

Second, a purpose/vision statement will vitalize the church. Paul Powell asks the question: Why do churches sit and die? He answers his own question by writing: (1) they lose their vision; (2) they lack sufficient faith; (3) and they refuse to change.[8] A well-written purpose statement will give your congregation new focus and new life.

Third, a purpose statement will help you develop your church's evangelistic zeal. In his book, *Building an Evangelistic Church,* Powell lists seven steps for building an evangelistic church:

1. Have a clear sense of purpose.
2. Pastor the people.
3. Build a warm and loving fellowship.
4. Develop an alive spirited worship.
5. Follow the time-tested laws of Sunday school growth.
6. Take a supermarket approach to ministry.
7. Have a passion for action.[9]

Notice the first step. Clarifying your purpose is always the place to begin.

Fourth, a good purpose statement clarifies the church's top priority. Churches determine their actions on the basis of priorities. These vary greatly from church to church. Rick Warren has listed some congregational priorities:

- *Tradition.* These congregations always ask, "What have we done in the past?"

- *Personality.* Churches like this ask, "What does the pastor want?" Or, if the church frequently changes pastors, "What does deacon X want?"

- *Finances.* A church that is money conscious will ask, "How much will it cost?"

- *Denomination.* A church that is denominationally focused will inquire, "What does the denomination want us to do?"

- *Seekers.* A seeker-driven church will desire to understand, "What do the unchurched want?" Warren insists that a church should be seeker-sensitive, not seeker-driven.[10]

Lyle Schaller observes that many churches forget outreach and focus on maintenance: "Every organization tends to move in the direction of defining purpose in terms of institutional maintenance and survival."[11] These churches focus on keeping the doors open, rather than bringing in the lost.

How can a church develop a purpose statement? The first step is to ask, "What is God's purpose for our church? Why do we exist?" Second, the church leaders should ask, "What does God want us to do in our locality?" Third, the church leaders should ask, "Whom should we target in our outreach?" This last question may surprise you. Surely every church should try to reach every lost person within its sphere of influence. In one way that is true; the church has the responsibility to see that all those folks hear the gospel. On the other hand, a single congregation cannot reach every type of person. Most churches have a distinct socioeconomic profile. If a church cannot reach a particular group of people, then it is the responsibility of that church to start a church or ministry to reach that group.

Many churches don't target a specific portion of the community, and they don't study those people in order to develop a strategy to reach them. They want to reach "people" for Christ, but they aren't clear as to which group or groups of people they can reach. Churches can target people geographically by pinpointing a particular neighborhood. Churches can also target demographically in targeting people by age, marital status, income, education, or occupation. It is also possible to target people according to language and culture.[12]

The New York church mentioned above targeted urban professionals. Willow Creek Church in Chicago targets baby boomers because they make up one-third of the population. Other churches plan to reach baby busters. I advised a pastor in Florida to target retired persons because they constituted a large portion of his town's population. Ethnic churches target people according to their language and culture. Your purpose statement ought to mention the people you plan to reach.

Your church is most likely to reach people who are like the members of your church. In other words, if your members are mainly professional people, then you will find it easier to reach professional people. If most of your members are elderly, you will likely find it difficult to reach baby busters. How can you determine your church's cultural profile? Ask these questions: Who already attends our church? What kind of leaders do we have? What groups in the community can the pastor relate to?[13]

The church's purpose statement should be clear, brief, and short enough to memorize. You will want to teach it to your people. If it is too long or complex, you will find it hard to communicate. Use action verbs in the statement; this is something you plan to *do*.

How can you communicate the purpose/vision statement? You and your church leaders may develop an excellent purpose statement, but it won't do your church any good unless your congregation understands it, approves it, and takes ownership of it. Sometimes pastors and leaders get too far ahead of their congregations. You may be excited, but are your followers? In order to accomplish your vision, you will have to get most of the members on board. Here are some ways you can communicate your vision for the church:

- *The pulpit.* You will want to preach on the church's general purpose and your church's specific purpose. The members of the congregation need to understand the biblical basis for the purpose statement and their pastor's vision for the church's future.

- *Conversations.* Take advantage of every opportunity to talk about the purpose statement. Engage as many members in conversation as possible. You want to get the people thinking about it.

- *Enlist influential leaders.* Every congregation has influential members. Typically, these are long-time members who have occupied positions of responsibility in the church. The pastor and members of the committee that composed the statement need to speak with these leaders individually and privately to gain their support.

- *Testimonies.* It is wise to enlist laypersons to give testimonies that will lead the congregation to approve the statement.

- *Mailings.* You will want to communicate the statement through the church bulletin and newsletter, but it is good to do a special mailing as well. You can hardly tell people something too often. One of my students works as a manager for United Parcel Service. He told me that the company assumes employees need to be told something seven times before they really learn it.

- *Congregational forums.* You may find it helpful to hold congregational forums—sessions where the people can ask questions and express their concerns.

- *Bulletin boards and banners.* If possible, develop a logo and a color scheme. Print your statement on banners and posters. Place these around the church so the people are sure to see them again and again.[14]

ANALYZE YOUR SITUATION

Research Your Community

Many church leaders know little about the community surrounding their church. I recently conducted a growth analysis for a church, and the leaders could not tell me the population of their town. If you expect to reach your community for Christ, you need to know as much about the community as possible. You need to know how many people live there, what their ethnic backgrounds are, what their income levels are, what their educational backgrounds are, and, what types of families compose the population. All of this data is collected by the Census Bureau and can help you develop a community profile. One of the few subject areas not covered by the Census Bureau is religious affiliation.

If your community is composed primarily of young families, your church will need to develop programs that minister to young families. If a significant percentage of the population is Hispanic, then you had better plan to offer some ministries using Spanish. For example, one of my students served a church in a rural area of Kentucky. When he surprisingly discovered a sizable community of Hispanics nearby, he immediately sought help and started Spanish-language Bible classes. This helped his church reach several families for Christ.

How can you acquire the data for your area? Many communities have a planning commission that keeps this data on file. Several commercial companies will prepare a community profile for a fee. School boards, public libraries, and chambers of commerce are also sources of information. Many denominations provide this data for their churches.

Another way to learn about your community is to talk with the people who live there. Before he launched his church-planting effort in Southern California, Rick Warren spoke with over one thousand people in their homes. He asked them what "other people" liked and disliked about churches. This dialogue helped him understand what kind of church could reach his target community. He then developed a profile (or description) of the type of person his church could reach. He planned his worship and sermons with this typical person in mind. This experience helped the church develop the principles of evangelism that have proved effective at Saddleback:

1. Know what you are fishing for!

2. Go where the fish are biting.

3. Learn to think like a fish!

4. Catch fish on their own terms—understand and adapt to their particular culture, understand their needs, understand their misconceptions.

5. Use more than one hook![15]

Analyze Your Church

A church planter can start from scratch, but most pastors inherit a situation. In order to reach a community for Christ, you need to know what your community is like, and you need to know what resources you have available to reach the community. Of course, you have the Holy Spirit to empower you, but you also have a congregation that can be mobilized for the task.

Every member in your church has received a spiritual gift, a gift from the Holy Spirit for building up the body of Christ. When the members learn, develop, and employ their spiritual gifts, the church will grow. You need to teach your people about spiritual gifts so they can discover their personal gift or gifts. Knowing their gifts is essential to planning.

You also need to do a talent survey. Ask the members about their educational backgrounds, talents, and experiences. This information will help you match resources with community needs.

SET SOME GOALS

Benefits of Goals

Once you have researched your community and analyzed your church, you are ready to set some goals for outreach. Why are goals necessary? Church growth experts always say, "If you aim at nothing, you are sure to hit it." That's for sure. Lots of churches set no goals, aim at nothing, and achieve nothing. Most older churches have no goals, only activities. Though churches may forget their original purpose, they continue to develop programs and plan meetings. Thus, churches may be active but not effective. Paul Powell says, "For a church to be strong, all its activities and programs must focus on winning and discipling people for Jesus Christ."[16]

Setting goals will help your church in the following ways:

- *Goals encourage members to commit themselves.* Setting goals will help motivate your members. They will work more enthusiastically and diligently if they believe they are accomplishing a worthy goal.

- *Goals provide specific direction.* Some churches are like the excited cowboy who rode off in all directions. These churches try to do too many things at one time. Goals focus your members' attention so that priority tasks are accomplished first.

- *Goals target specific needs.* All churches face limitless needs. We can't do everything for everyone all the time. Goals help the church focus on particular needs.

- *Goals enhance evaluation.* If you develop a list of specific goals, you can evaluate your progress better. Evaluation helps you make the "mid-course" adjustments that are almost always necessary in any project or program.[17]

- *Goals help you accomplish more.* Setting goals helps you achieve more than you would without them. One church set a goal of 250 for high attendance day in Sunday school, but only reached 214. At first the pastor was discouraged because the goal was not met. When he discovered that 214 was the highest attendance in twenty-three years, he said, "We did not meet our goal, but the goal helped us achieve more than we would have otherwise."

Qualities of Good Goals

Developing appropriate goals is an essential part of the planning process. Good goals reflect these qualities:

- *A good goal must be a faith goal.* A good goal challenges your people to work hard and trust God. They should be able to see that the goal cannot be reached without God's help.

- *A good goal is developed through prayer.* Goals should only be set after much prayer. God's guidance is essential in developing goals that will motivate church members and fulfill the Great Commission.

- *A good goal is measurable.* A goal should be measurable. If it isn't, it will be hard to know whether you achieved it or not. It is fine to desire that your people "grow in Christ," but how will you know if they do or not? Just set a goal like this: "Every adult Sunday school teacher will complete the *Experiencing God* study within one year." You will know if you achieve this goal. It's specific. It's measurable. A pastor might say, "My goal is to grow our Sunday school this year." That is a rather vague goal. It is better to phrase the goal like this: "Our goal is to increase Sunday school enrollment by 40 percent during this calendar year." A good goal is specific and measurable.

- *A good goal is manageable.* A goal should challenge your members to do more than they have done before. Remember my son Micah, the football player? During the off-season he lifts weights. Every day he tries to lift a little more. The coaches insist that he increase his lifting capacity by small increments. In the same way, wise church leaders set goals that challenge their people but do not discourage them. I've seen overenthusiastic pastors set goals that were too ambitious; they were so high that church members did not even try to reach them. Your goal should be within the realm of possibility.

- *A good goal is owned by the members.* If the members of the church personally commit to accomplishing a goal, they will work harder. I've seen a lot of pastors set goals, but the members did little to achieve them. They didn't believe in the goals, so they weren't motivated to work to achieve them. If people have a part in setting the goal, they will be more likely to work to achieve it.

- *A good goal is written.* Writing the goal is a good way to clarify it and make it concrete. Presenting your evangelism goals in black and white is a key to promoting them.

- *A good goal is relevant.* Every goal you set should clearly contribute to achieving the church's purpose that gives birth to the goals in the first place.

DEVELOP ACTION PLANS

Setting goals is important, but goals don't accomplish themselves. You have to make plans to achieve them. A football coach has a clear goal—win the game. His game plan details how the players can accomplish that goal. Your plans will help you achieve the goals God has guided you to set.

An action plan answers these questions:

- What will be accomplished?
- Who will do this?
- When will this be done?
- Where will it be done?
- How will it be done?
- What resources are required?

You may find it helpful to develop printed forms that lay out the action plan. These forms will help ensure that all essential factors are considered.

Here's an example. You want to conduct a witness training program for your lay leaders. You designate someone as the coordinator and decide what type of training to offer. Then you choose someone to teach the sessions. Next you calendar the training event and decide where to conduct the training. Finally, you will have to prepare a budget. Of course, all of this will have to be approved by the appropriate body in your church.

EVALUATE THE RESULTS

As your plans progress, you will want to evaluate them periodically. Very few plans develop exactly the way you lay them out. Most require some adjustment. You may also want to build some flexibility into the plan. For instance, let's say you've planned a picnic and encouraged your members to invite lost friends. You would do well to have a Plan B in case of rain.

It's also important to evaluate programs and projects after they are completed. You may want to survey the participants to get their reactions. You and other leaders need to go over the process to see what could be done better the next time. Finally, you will need to assess the results to see if they are worth the time, money, and effort expended. Someone might say, "Even one saved person is worth any cost." That is certainly true; but as our time and money are limited, we must be good stewards of both. Is it best to continue to use moderately effective methods when other methods might win more people to Christ? Honest evaluation will help you decide whether to use a particular method again.

CELEBRATE VICTORIES

When a project or program is successfully completed, celebrate the results. Make a lot out of every success, however small. When our children were learning to walk, we encouraged them by rejoicing over every step. Thus encouraged, they kept trying until they could walk and run. You may have to praise baby steps in a declining church; however, if you celebrate little victories, you will soon be celebrating big ones.

If you praise your workers, they will work harder in the future. If a visitation worker wins someone to Christ, rejoice and praise the worker. If a class meets its high attendance goal, honor the class and recognize the achievement. Look for victories to celebrate. Churches that have been plateaued or declining for some time need all the encouragement you can give them.

CALENDAR EVANGELISTIC EVENTS

One way to make evangelism intentional is to develop a specific calendar. This calendar will help you ensure that evangelism is prioritized. I suggest that small- and medium-sized churches have one evangelistic event or emphasis each month. Larger churches may want to have more. Here is a sample calendar:

January–Have a soul-winning commitment day.

February–Take a group to an evangelism conference.

March–Conduct a lay evangelism school.

April–Promote High-Attendance Day on Easter. Hold a spring revival.

May–Sponsor a bring-a-friend day.

June–Conduct Vacation Bible School; follow up on prospects.

July–Take youth to camp; speak with each about salvation.

August–Conduct backyard Bible clubs. Sponsor an evangelistic concert in the park.

September–Conduct evangelism training for Sunday school teachers.

October–Hold a high-attendance Sunday.

November–Conduct an evangelism training program for youth.

December–Present a Christmas pageant with an evangelistic impact.[18]

These events are just suggestions, but I'm sure you get the idea. Making an evangelism calendar will ensure a year-round emphasis on evangelism.

SUMMARY

Churches must intend to reach people for Christ. This intentional effort is important because it resists the tendency to let up on evangelism. The first step in planning for church evangelism is to clarify your church's mission and purpose. Once you have written your purpose statement, you can develop some specific goals to accomplish the purpose. When you have a set of goals, you can prepare action plans in order to achieve your goals. As you implement your plans, you will want to assess the results. Correct the plan as necessary. Finally, celebrate victories and successes. These celebrations will motivate your people to work hard in the future. A church evangelism calendar will help you maintain a year-long emphasis on evangelism.

STUDY QUESTIONS

1. Why is it important to plan a church's evangelism program?

2. What is the difference between a church mission statement and a vision statement?

3. What are the qualities of a good goal?

4. What questions will an action plan answer?

5. Why is it important to celebrate successes?

6. Why is an evangelism calendar advantageous?

FOR FURTHER STUDY

Barna, George. *The Power of Vision.* Ventura, Calif.: Regal Books, 1992.

Powell, Paul. *Building an Evangelistic Church.* Dallas: Annuity Board, 1991.

Robinson, Darrell W. *Total Church Life.* Nashville: Broadman Press, 1993.

Shrum, Ron. "Goal Setting and Church Growth." *Growing Churches* (January-March 1992): 28–29.

Wright, C. Thomas, ed. *Church Evangelism Council Manual.* Atlanta: Home Mission Board, 1993.

CHAPTER 6

MOBILIZE THE CONGREGATION

❯❯ ———————— ❮❮

Growing churches involve a higher percentage of their members in outreach and ministry than stagnant or declining churches. A pastor, or even a pastor and staff, cannot reach the church's community for Christ. Many church members try to place the responsibility for outreach on the pastor alone, but this is unbiblical and impractical. A church functioning like this is like a basketball team in which the coach plays and the players cheer. No coach, no matter how athletic, could win a game like that. One reason why many churches are declining is because they fail to use all their resources.

INVOLVE THE LAITY

Here are ten good reasons why you should emphasize lay involvement:

1. *Involving laypersons is the biblical model.* Ephesians 4:11–12 clarifies this point. The Holy Spirit provides missionaries, evangelists, prophets, and pastors to the church for an express purpose: to equip church members for ministry. Pastors in particular must give priority to equipping members for ministry. The ministry belongs to all God's people, not just pastors and staff members. Several biblical analogies illustrate this shared ministry. Jesus said; "I am the vine, you are the

branches" (John 15:5). The branches are the part of the tree that produce the fruit. Similarly, Jesus described himself as the Good Shepherd (John 10). No shepherd produces wool; the sheep do that. The shepherd works to create the proper conditions so the sheep can gain the most weight and grow the most wool. Their productivity demonstrates the shepherd's competence.

2. *Involving laypersons is the historical model.* Several years ago I did extensive research on evangelism in the early church. As I read, the accounts of early lay evangelists impressed me greatly. In the early church two deacons, Philip and Stephen, preached powerful evangelistic messages. When Saul scattered the Jerusalem church, the Christians shared the gospel wherever they went (Acts 8:4). In fact, these Christian refugees founded the great missionary church at Antioch. Christianity spread throughout the Roman Empire primarily through the witness of merchants and soldiers.

The story of Aedesius and Frumentius provides us with one of the most interesting stories of lay evangelism. Early in the fourth century these two young men were shipwrecked on the coast of Axum (Ethiopia). The locals rescued them and the king made them his household slaves. Like Joseph before them, they soon won the king's favor and achieved prominence in the kingdom. The king gave them full freedom to preach, and they soon won many converts. After several years the king permitted them to return home. Aedesius returned directly to their home in Tyre, but Frumentius visited Bishop Athanasius in Alexandria and appealed for priests to serve the church in Axum. Athanasius replied, "Who could be found more suitable than yourself?" and immediately ordained him as bishop. Frumentius returned to Axum and served there until his death.[1]

3. *Involving laypersons provides for the multiplication of converts rather than the addition of converts.* The world's population grows geometrically rather than arithmetically (2-4-8-16-32 rather than 1+1+1+1+1). Therefore, we must employ an evangelistic strategy that will multiply disciples geometrically. The only way to do this is to develop disciples who can reproduce themselves spiritually. Paul wrote of this in 2 Timothy 2:2, "And the

things you have heard me say in the presence of many witnesses entrust to reliable men who will also be qualified to teach others."

4. *Involving laypersons is a good stewardship of time.* A veteran missionary once told me, "It's better to train ten people to do the work, than to try to do the work of ten people." He was absolutely right. A basic principle of pastoral leadership is this: Train the members to do what they can, and you do what they can't.

5. *Involving laypersons helps the pastor avoid burnout.* Many pastors burn out after several years in the ministry. Though several factors contribute to this, almost all pastors suffering from burnout have been trying to do everything themselves. By delegating responsibilities in the church, pastors can reduce their stress level and maybe even spend an occasional evening with their families. When I met the mother of ten children, I wondered how she managed her household. Then I observed her in action. Her method was obvious. She trained the older children to help her do the chores and mind the little ones. If she had tried to do everything herself, she wouldn't have survived a month. Mom supervised, but she didn't try to do everything herself.

6. *Involving the laity helps to develop a mature, well-rounded church.* A veteran pastor told me, "The measure of a pastorate is how well the church functions when the pastor leaves. If the church falls apart, the pastor failed. If the church prospers, that pastor did a good job." Wise pastors develop lay leaders; unwise pastors orient everything around themselves. A mature church needs trained, capable lay leaders.

7. *Involving laypersons shares the ministry and the blessing.* Ministering to others blesses the minister as well as the person being ministered to. When laypeople fail to participate in the church's ministries, they miss out on many blessings. Pastors need to share the ministry and the accompanying blessings.

8. *Involving laypersons helps them mature spiritually.* Children need to exercise in order to grow strong. Young Christians need exercise, too—physical exercise and spiritual exercise. Every

believer needs to serve in and through the church; otherwise they will always be weak.

9. *Involving laypersons can start web movements.* Donald McGavran coined the term *web movement* to refer to the web of relationships that all people have—kinships, friendships, and social networks of all kinds. Every person you win to Christ can be the beginning of a web movement for Christ. That person can witness to friends and relatives and bring them into the church's sphere of influence.

10. *Training lay workers follows Christ's example.* Jesus spent much of his time training his disciples. Wise pastors will follow his example.

MOTIVATE THE MEMBERS

Most pastors want to involve their people in ministry, but experience has shown them that many people are simply unwilling to be part of the ministry of the church. What factors "de-motivate" people; that is, what keeps them from serving in the church as they ought?

Hindrances to Service

You probably remember the assertion made earlier that churches will naturally grow if they are unhindered. Every pastor and staff member must examine their congregation carefully to identify and remove obstacles that hinder their members' service to God. Here are some common hindrances:

"Subbiblical" theology. Many members do not believe in the lostness of humanity or the reality of hell. They are universalists, believing that ultimately all will be saved. If one believes this, there truly is no point in outreach efforts.

Fear. I'm convinced that many want to share the gospel, but they are afraid to do so. They may fear rejection or embarrassment; but whatever the case, they will not become involved because of fear.

Ignorance. Others hesitate to become involved because they don't know what to do or say. They could be activated through training.

Burnout. I've met many people who once served actively in the church, but were overused (or abused). When the Nominating Committee recognized their commitment, they gave them every job that came open. They accepted the jobs but found that they could not maintain such a fast pace; eventually they quit doing anything. What a shame! We need to see our service for God as a marathon, not a sprint. We need to help members find a pace they can maintain for a lifetime.

Physical incapacity. If you visit shut-ins, you'll find many saints who once served faithfully. Now, however, they are physically incapable of working.

Feelings of inadequacy. Some believers have such a low self-image, and such a lack of self-confidence, that they may hesitate to accept responsibility.

Hurt feelings. Some members served in the past, but they were criticized for something. This hurt their feelings, and now they refuse to do anything.

Lack of commitment. Some believers are immature in their faith and lacking in commitment.

Lack of time. This is the most common reason given for not serving. For some this is just an excuse, but for some it's really true. In the past, married women did much of the volunteer work in the church. Now, however, many wives and mothers work outside the home. The time they have available for ministry truly is lacking. Also, many corporations have downsized, forcing the remaining employees to work longer hours.

Unclear roles. Many church members do not know what their spiritual gifts are, and they don't have a clue about what they should do in the church.

Frustration. Some members have become frustrated in their work in the church because they have served in the wrong capacity. Nominating committees typically are more concerned about staffing programs than they are with helping people serve according to their spiritual gifts. When folks are asked to serve in an assignment for which they aren't gifted, they quickly become frustrated. Other believers wanted to develop a ministry or do a project, but their plans were thwarted. They, too, have quit in frustration.

Unchallenged. Amazingly, some members have never been asked to serve. If they were approached in the right way and given proper training, they could and would serve effectively.

Once you have identified the hindrance to service, you can devise ways to eliminate them. I strongly believe that teaching on spiritual gifts and training for service can greatly increase the number of people serving in our churches.

Types of Motivation

In most churches, 20 percent of the people do 80 percent of the work. How can we activate the 80 percent? Obviously, these people need to be motivated. But how? How can a pastor motivate people to work in the church's outreach program? Here is a list of some factors that motivate people:

guilt	goals	love
fear	thrill	security
money	success	helping people
fame	prestige	being the best
power	recognition	better life[2]

Some motivators are nobler than others. Pastors tend to motivate their people by emphasizing guilt or duty. Guilt is a powerful factor. Perhaps you've heard preachers tell their congregations that the blood of the lost is on their hands because they failed to warn them of coming judgment (Ezek. 33:6). Oh yes, you *can* use guilt to motivate people, but not for long. Its power decreases rapidly. Duty endures longer, but it is not the best motivator.

Kenneth Gangel has listed several reasons why people volunteer to serve in the church.

- They want to be needed:
- They want to help others and make a difference.
- They want to learn new skills and to use the skills they have already learned.
- They want to feel accepted in a caring community.
- They want self-esteem and affirmation.
- They want to grow in their faith and use spiritual gifts.
- They want to avoid loneliness.
- They want to support a cause they believe in.[3]

In practice most people serve out of mixed motives. Few serve for a single reason. It's important for you to discern what motivates different members and to treat them accordingly. I once read an interview with Sparky Anderson, a highly successful baseball manager. He said that some players need encouragement, while some need a kick in the pants. The trick to managing is knowing who needs what and when.

The best motivator is *love.* Jesus understood this. When Jesus spoke with Peter after his resurrection, he asked three times, "Do you truly love me?" (John 21:15). Twice Peter answered "yes." The third time he declared, "Lord, you know all things; you know that I love you" (John 21:17). To which Jesus replied, "Feed my sheep." And Peter did just that. Peter the coward became Peter the lion, and he served faithfully until his death in Nero's persecution. The best way to motivate people is to challenge them to demonstrate their love for Christ.[4]

Methods of Motivation

People can and will do what they are motivated to do. I heard about a woman who was asked to teach in her church's Vacation Bible School. She refused, saying she didn't have enough time. Then her husband won a trip to Hawaii. Somehow she managed to find time to go with him on the trip. People will do what they want to do. How can you lead them to want to work in your church's outreach ministry?

Information. John Bisagno, pastor of the First Baptist Church in Houston, Texas, emphasizes the importance of *information.* He says, "Information plus motivation equals action." Church members can't respond to a need if they don't know it exists. However, most members know they ought to be involved in outreach, but they aren't. They need a changed attitude. I've been involved with athletic teams for many years, first as a player, and now as a coach or trainer. Attitude makes all the difference. Even mediocre teams can do well if they develop a winning attitude.

Enthusiasm. We can change our people's attitude and improve their motivation by demonstrating *enthusiasm.* If you want your people to get excited, you must be excited first. The word *enthusiasm* comes from two Greek words, *en* and *theos.* It means "in God" or "God in you." That is what we need: God in us. We need the Holy Spirit to move pastors and their congregations. The early church didn't need seminars on motivation; the Holy Spirit filled the believers, and they boldly proclaimed the gospel. Pray that both you and your people will be filled with holy enthusiasm.

Repetition. You can also motivate people through repetition. Advertisers build interest in their products through repetition. If you want your people to be more involved in evangelism and outreach, you need to emphasize it repeatedly. You can accentuate evangelism through your sermons, announcements, newsletter column, and private conversations.

Illustration. You should take every opportunity to motivate by illustration. When you preach, mention someone in the church who has done something good, especially in outreach. When you introduce new members, ask the outreach worker who contacted those persons to stand with them. Ask new believers to give their testimonies in the worship service. Seeing their joy will motivate your members to witness more often.

Example. Motivate your people by your personal example. They won't witness or visit more than you do. You must set the pace. I spoke with a staff member of a church that had fifty men making visits every Saturday morning. I asked how they were able to get such a good turnout. He said, "They know that the pastor will be here every Saturday. He doesn't tell them; he leads them."[5]

Patience. Let me add a word of caution here. If your church has not been active in outreach for awhile, it may take some time to get it moving again. Don't be discouraged if you have poor attendance at visitation the first few weeks. If you begin a visitation program, and only two people come to visit, that's all right. That is two more than you had before! Work with those who have concern for the lost and a will to reach out. Jesus began with just a few, and so can you.

ENLIGHTEN THE MEMBERS

In order to serve effectively, your people need to discover their spiritual gifts. Most Christians serve in frustration and futility because they are doing the wrong thing. Too often we put square pegs in round holes. I always enjoy watching the coaches at the beginning of football season. They spend the first two weeks determining who can play the different positions. They know that correct assignments are the key to success. This is why they run the players through all kinds of drills to assess their speed, strength, and aggressiveness. They want to find which players have soft hands and which players have hands of stone. As a pastor you must determine where your members can best serve. The way to begin this process is by teaching them about spiritual gifts.

The gifts of the Holy Spirit are special abilities given to you to serve in and through the church. Gifts are different from talents. Talents are natural abilities that God gives us at birth, and they should be used for the benefit of Christ's church. The Holy Spirit gives us spiritual gifts at our second birth, when we're born again. Each believer receives at least one spiritual gift (1 Cor. 12:7). The Holy Spirit gives us these gifts so that we can build up the body of Christ (1 Cor. 12:7). Adrian Rogers says, "The gifts are given for employment, not enjoyment." He means that they are given for practical reasons, not for our pleasure.

There are many different gifts of the Holy Spirit. I believe the lists of gifts found in the New Testament are illustrative, not exhaustive. They show the types of gifts the Holy Spirit gives, but they do not list all gifts. Not all gifts are equally important (1 Cor. 12:31), and everyone does not receive the same gift. The Holy Spirit gives gifts according to the needs of the church. Churches need people with different gifts just as a basketball team needs different kinds of players. If a team had all point guards, who would rebound? Or, if the team was composed of nothing but centers, who would bring the ball up the court against the press? The Holy Spirit knows what each church needs and gifts the members accordingly.

Three passages in the New Testament deal with spiritual gifts: 1 Corinthians 12–14, Romans 12, and Ephesians 4. There are many different ways to categorize the gifts. This is the way I do it:

Empathizing

Serving (Rom. 12:7)
Giving (Rom. 12:8)
Leading (Rom. 12:8)
Mercy (Rom. 12:8)

Evangelism

Apostle (Eph. 4:11)
Evangelist (Eph. 4:11)
Pastor/Teacher (Eph. 4:11)

Encouragement

Teaching (Rom. 12:7)

Encouraging (Rom. 12:8)

Faith (1 Cor. 12:9)

Discernment (1 Cor. 12:10)

Wisdom (1 Cor. 12:8)

Knowledge (1 Cor. 12:8)

Energizing

Prophecy (Rom. 12:6)

Miracles (1 Cor. 12:28)

Tongues (1 Cor. 12:28)

Interpretations (1 Cor. 12:30)

Healing (1 Cor. 12:28)

Pastors need to help their members discover their spiritual gifts. There are a number of booklets and questionnaires available to expedite this. Or, you can develop your own approach. As you walk your members through the process, you will want to encourage them to follow these steps:

1. Acknowledge the source of the gift.

2. Study the Scripture passages.

3. Pray for the Spirit's guidance.

4. Ask for wise counsel.

5. Experiment in different areas.

6. Develop your gift through training.

7. Use your gift to strengthen the church.

8. Thank God for the privilege of serving.

The basic idea here is to help your members understand how God has gifted them. This understanding will help guide them to the ministry in the church where they can serve most effectively. For too long, our churches have been program-driven rather than gifts-driven. When believers understand their spiritual identity, they can minister effectively. The diagram on page 83 may help you visualize the process.

ENLIST MEMBERS FOR OUTREACH

It isn't easy to enlist members for evangelistic outreach. Even the idea of witnessing scares many Christians. If you want to reach your

Figure 6.1

community, however, you will have to recruit an outreach team. How can you recruit effective workers? Calvin Ratz makes six suggestions:

1. *Preach on lay involvement in outreach.* Make a fervent appeal for workers. These appeals may not generate much response, but at least you will sensitize the congregation.

2. *Pray for recruits.* Jesus prayed all night before he selected his disciples. In Matthew 9:38 Jesus commanded us to "ask the Lord of the harvest, therefore, to send out workers into his harvest field." Pray and ask God to bring to mind members who could serve effectively in outreach.

3. *Enlist new converts.* New converts possess enthusiasm that veteran Christians don't usually have. Harness that power for

outreach. Also, new converts can reach new networks of people for Christ.

4. *Enlist people personally.* Jesus personally called his disciples to follow him. If the pastor personally asks a member to do something, the person will usually do it. Appeals from the pulpit will never be as effective as personal requests.

5. *Enlist people for specific tasks with time limits.* Clearly spell out what you are asking the person to do and how long it will take. Also, recognize the fact that some people are willing to do some things but not others. Let them do what they are willing to do.

6. *Enlist the entire congregation for lifestyle evangelism.* Organized visitation programs are important, but the most valuable witnessing is done in the course of daily life. Lifestyle (or friendship) evangelism should be an ongoing concern for the whole congregation. Train all the members of the church to seize the opportunities that arise day to day.[6]

TRAIN YOUR MEMBERS

Jesus' Principles of Training

Trained workers are essential to any outreach program. Many people stop working in the church because they were never trained to do their tasks. How many new Sunday school teachers have been given a quarterly and told to go teach? Obviously, Jesus knew the importance of training his disciples. He spent three years doing it. How can you train your members?

Begin by learning how Jesus trained his own disciples. Here are the steps he followed:

- Step One—Jesus chose men who were seeking the kingdom of God, had big hearts, and were teachable.

- Step Two—Jesus modeled ministry. He showed them what he wanted them to do.

- Step Three—Jesus spent lots of time with his disciples. This is the principle of association. Jesus wanted his followers to catch his vision and methods.

- Step Four—Jesus taught his disciples to pray. Your workers must learn to pray for power and guidance.

- Step Five—Jesus taught his disciples by word and demonstration. Much of what we read in the four Gospels is Jesus' instruction of the disciples. If you want someone to do something, teach him how to do it.

- Step Six—Jesus provided the needed resources by giving his disciples the Holy Spirit, the Scriptures, and his own presence. Be sure your workers have what they need to serve effectively.

- Step Seven—Jesus sent his disciples out. Jesus knew they would learn by doing, and he gave them a chance to practice what they had observed and heard.

- Step Eight—Jesus evaluated and affirmed his disciples. When the disciples returned from their preaching trip, Jesus praised them for their good work. When you send your people out, let them share the results with you. Praise them for their efforts and make suggestions for improvement.[7]

Methods of Training

There are many ways to train your members for evangelism. You will probably want to use several of them. Variety is important in training for evangelism because different approaches appeal to different people. Personality types play some part in this. Also, different methods are appropriate at different times. With a new neighbor you might use friendship evangelism, but you wouldn't want to use that method with a dying hospital patient.

You may want to adopt one of the programs of personal evangelism. *Continuing Witness Training* and its cousin, *Evangelism Explosion,* are sixteen-week programs that provide intensive training in evangelism. Another new program is called *People Sharing Jesus;* it is more relational in its orientation. You might decide to hold a one- or two-day evangelism seminar to get things going.[8]

Most vocational evangelists are ready and willing to lead an evangelistic training event. Often they have free time in the winter and summer months. I can personally assure you that many seminary professors would also be glad to assist you. Furthermore, parachurch organizations like Campus Crusade for Christ and the Navigators have produced fine materials for use in churches.

Many Christian camps and conference centers sponsor evangelism conferences and training seminars. Denominational organizations sponsor training events each year. You can expose your people to wonderful training through videotapes. The main thing here is to do something. If your church is small, renting or borrowing a set of videotaped lessons may be the way to go. Or, you might contact some other pastors in your area to see if they would like to cooperate in a training event.

As you plan your training, keep these things in mind.

- Provide some kind of training every year.

- Budget for training. Training and retraining your workers should be a high priority.

- Schedule the sessions carefully. I once spoke at a church on the night of the local high school's football homecoming game. Five people attended the meeting, counting the pastor and his wife.

- Promote the meeting extensively. You will need to personally invite key people you want to attend.

- Be sure that your training program includes actual witnessing. There is no substitute for on-the-job training in evangelism.

PRAISE YOUR WORKERS

Praise and affirm those who serve in the outreach program. You will draw more workers with praise than with guilt. If you praise those who get involved, the others will catch the vision. If you read Paul's Epistles, you'll notice that he always began with thanksgiving and praise for the saints. That is a good example for you to follow.

SUMMARY

If you want to reach your community for Christ, you must involve your laypeople. You can't do it alone. You can motivate them to serve by emphasizing evangelism in your sermons and by setting a good personal example. A wise pastor helps the people discover their spiritual gifts so they can serve with more effectiveness and satisfaction. A key to enlisting people for service is a personal appeal. Once you have enlisted some workers, train them to evangelize. Renew their training every year. Finally, praise them for their efforts.

STUDY QUESTIONS

1. In your opinion, what are the three most significant factors that hinder people from working in the church?
2. Why is love a better motivating factor than guilt?
3. What are four keys to motivating people?
4. What are the six principles for enlisting workers?
5. How did Jesus train his disciples?

FOR FURTHER STUDY

Gangel, Kenneth O. *Feeding and Leading.* Wheaton: Victor Books, 1989.

George, Carl F. and Robert Logan. *Leading and Managing Your Church.* Grand Rapids: Fleming H. Revell, 1987.

Hemphill, Ken. *The Antioch Effect.* Nashville: Broadman & Holman, 1994.

McDonough, Reginald M. *Keys to Effective Motivation.* Nashville: Broadman Press, 1979.

Ratz, Calvin, Frank Tillapaugh, and Myron Augsburger. *Mastering Outreach and Evangelism.* Portland: Multnomah Press, 1990.

GROW THROUGH GROUPS

➤ ———————— ◄

Small groups are essential to church outreach and growth. Growing churches all over the world use small groups to win people to Christ and to disciple them. From the huge Yoido Full Gospel Church in Seoul to the New Hope Community Church in Portland, pastors have discovered that small groups can be an effective evangelistic tool. They call these groups by many names—cell groups, home Bible fellowships, tender loving care groups. No matter what they are called, small groups can aid church growth.

Small groups are nothing new. The Pietists thrived on cottage prayer meetings. John Wesley encouraged his converts in methodist "classes." Southern Baptists have used Sunday school classes as a primary outreach tool for years, but the emphasis on off-campus groups is relatively recent. Robert Wuthnow of Princeton University studied the small group boom and discovered that 40 percent of Americans participate in at least one small group. Almost 60 percent of American Protestants are active in a group. According to Wuthnow, there are 900,000 Bible study groups, 800,000 adult Sunday school classes, 750,000 special interest groups, and 500,000 self-help groups in the United States.[1]

Why do people join small groups? Wuthnow reports that 73 percent join in order to grow personally. Others join because friends invited them. Forty-three percent join because they learn about the group at their church. Kennon Callahan says that people join small groups because they are searching for community. He defines community as "a group of people in which significant relationships of sharing and caring can take place."[2]

It is important to understand that churches are actually collections of groups. A very small church might be composed of just one group, but most churches are a collection of congregations that share the same physical facilities and staff. Growing congregations recognize the need for community and provide opportunities for people to participate in different kinds of groups.

Growing churches must continue to start new groups. These groups are especially important for new members and prospects. New people will join new groups, but many find it difficult or awkward to join established groups. Established groups tend to bond so closely that new people cannot break into them. It is easier for new members to establish meaningful relationships with each other when the group's network of relationships is still open and pliable. For this reason, growing churches continually start new groups. In fact, Kennon Callahan goes so far as to declare, "Those churches that quit starting new groups are churches that have decided to die."[3]

Small groups not only attract new members; they also help churches to retain members. My friend Chip Miller, Sunday School director for the Kentucky Baptist Convention, says that people stay in a church for three reasons. First, they believe their faith is being nurtured. Second, they feel a sense of belonging to a group in the church. Third, they feel a sense of ownership in their church–this is *my church.* Obviously, small groups and Sunday school classes can help in all three of these areas.

TEN ADVANTAGES OF SMALL GROUPS

Small groups can enhance your evangelistic efforts. They offer these advantages:

1. *The small group setting is nonthreatening.* Many people are intimidated by church buildings, but a neighbor's living room is not threatening to them.

2. *No special facility is required.* Small groups can meet in homes, offices, schools, and restaurants. In New Testament times,

believers met wherever it was convenient, and that is also true of small groups.

3. *The casual atmosphere is attractive.* Small groups don't require any special knowledge or clothing. Some folks hesitate to attend "church" because they don't know what to do or what to wear. How many times have you invited someone to church, and the person replied, "I don't have the right clothes"?

4. *The small group provides intimacy.* In small groups people relate to one another on a personal level. People want to participate in a group where people know their names and miss them when they are absent.

5. *The interaction and group participation allow people to find answers to their questions.* Many adults have questions about the Bible and other religious matters. They can't ask the preacher during a sermon, but they can ask their small-group leader.

6. *Small groups have flexible scheduling.* It would be hard to reschedule a worship service for a congregation of six hundred members, but a small group can easily adjust its meeting time.

7. *Small groups can emphasize the Bible.* Not all small groups are Bible study groups, but many are. They provide an opportunity for verse-by-verse study of the Scriptures. Most of these groups employ inductive Bible study methods that encourage people to discover spiritual truths in the context of group discussion.

8. *The emphasis on Bible study provides a good biblical foundation for those making decisions for Christ.* When people profess Christ in a small group, the group leader has a good reading on that person's level of spiritual understanding. When someone makes a decision in an evangelistic meeting or worship service, it is often difficult to ascertain the person's sincerity and understanding. However, those who make decisions in a small group are more likely to be biblically informed. You can be more confident that they know what they are doing. People have to understand that they are lost before they can be saved. When a person professes Christ after several weeks of Bible study, you can be more certain he understands what he is doing.

9. *The small group provides a natural system of follow-up for those who make commitments to Christ.* The follow-up and retention of converts is a continual problem for the church. When I was a missionary, we were pleased if we baptized 20 percent of the people who made decisions in an evangelistic crusade. However, those who profess Christ in connection with a small group are already involved with a support group. The members of the group will encourage them and support them in their newfound faith.

10. *In church-planting situations, small groups develop naturally into churches.* Both home and foreign missionaries use small groups as a way to plant new churches. The Bible study group grows and becomes a worship fellowship. Eventually, the fellowship is constituted as a church.[4]

TYPES OF SMALL GROUPS

Cell Group

A cell group is a Bible study and fellowship group for adults that meets away from the church. Many churches encourage their members to participate in a cell group. Cell groups provide Bible study, fellowship, worship, and care for their members. Typically, these groups meet once a week in their small group and gather with the other cell groups for worship on Sundays. Ralph Neighbour Jr. has written extensively on cell groups, and he lists these advantages:

1. *Cell groups are like the New Testament churches.* The New Testament churches met in homes.

2. *Cells group do not require a building.* Church buildings are expensive, and they are normally used only a few hours each week. Cell groups can meet anywhere, and their number can expand at no expense.

3. *Cell groups emphasize prayer.*

4. *Cell groups are the ideal way to penetrate the world's cities.* The traditional building-oriented church is not a financially feasible option in many major cities because the cost of land and buildings makes this model impossible to implement. However, cell groups can be started and multiply infinitely because they do not require special facilities.

5. *Cell groups do not have to keep a schedule.* Most Sunday school classes operate on a fixed schedule. They usually meet only for one hour each week, some for forty-five minutes. Because of its flexible scheduling, a cell group can meet for a longer time.

6. *Cell groups can evangelize their neighborhoods.* Most cell groups are organized by neighborhoods. These groups can reach their neighbors for Christ.[5]

The best-known cell group church is the Yoido Full Gospel Church in Seoul, Korea. Thousands of cell groups meet all over Seoul. Pastor Yonggi Cho started this church in a tent with five members in 1958. Now the church has almost one million members. Pastor Cho is a dynamic preacher, but he freely admits that the key to the church's growth is the cell group.[6]

The New Hope Community Church is probably the largest cell group church in the United States. Dale Galloway planted the church in 1972. By 1990, weekly worship attendance averaged six thousand. Galloway says the breakthrough came when he discovered the 20/20 Vision. He derived this vision from Acts 20:20, where Paul described his house-to-house ministry in Ephesus. In 1990, New Hope sponsored 450 Tender Loving Care groups. These are cell groups led by laypersons. The lay leaders receive instruction and guidance from district pastors. All the members worship together at the Saturday night and Sunday morning services. Galloway says the result is "an organization with no internal limits to its ability to keep expanding."[7]

Sunday School

The Sunday school class is the most common and familiar type of small group. Some church growth writers have written off the Sunday school and stressed the need for small (or cell) groups that meet away from the church building. Many of these writers are unfamiliar with the evangelistic Sunday schools conducted by independent and Southern Baptist churches. They think of Sunday school only as an organization that spiritually nurtures children.

Actually, a Sunday school is a collection of small groups that meet at the same time and place. A Sunday school class functions much like a cell group. Notice the tasks of the Sunday school:

- *Reach* people;
- *Teach* the Bible;
- *Witness* to the unsaved;
- *Minister* to people's needs;
- *Lead* people to worship;
- *Tell* members about the work of the church and denomination.

These tasks are the same as those of a cell group. It seems to me that churches need both Sunday school and cell groups. We want to increase the number of entrance points into the church. One way to do this is to organize new Sunday school classes and new cell groups.

The cell-group approach is a good model to use, especially in urban areas. If you are starting a church from scratch, give serious consideration to using the cell-group model. However, it is almost impossible to convert a traditional church into a cell-group church. If you are serving a traditional church, you may want to add small groups to your church program. However, you will want to maintain your Sunday school. With some effort you can revitalize your Sunday school and make it an effective evangelistic and outreach tool.

Some church growth experts like Thom Rainer and Ken Hemphill believe the Sunday school is superior to cell groups, at least in the United States. Hemphill has listed the advantages of Sunday School:

1. *Sunday school is statistically more effective.* An effective cell-group church can expect to have 25 percent of its worshipers participate in a cell group. The average Southern Baptist church had 80.6 percent of its worshipers attend Sunday school in 1993.

2. *The age-graded Sunday school is easier to organize and administer.*

3. *The Sunday school is less likely to become personality-oriented.*

4. *Sunday school's consistent curriculum makes it easier to protect doctrinal integrity.* Classes that meet in one place and at one time are easier to monitor.

5. *Sunday school reinforces worship because it meets before or after worship.*

6. *Sunday school emphasizes total family biblical education.* During Sunday school, the whole family studies the Bible at the same time. Cell groups tend to be just for adults.[8]

As you've read, there is still a lot to be said for the Sunday school. Some churches that emphasize small groups have been forced to establish Sunday schools to meet the needs of children and young people. Actually, the dichotomy between cell groups and Sunday school is a false one. Cell groups and Sunday school can coexist; they can even complement each other. You may reach some adults through cell groups who can then be funneled into the regular church program.

Fellowship Groups

Many churches have established fellowship groups. The impetus for these came from the Lay Renewal Movement. Fellowship groups usually do not intend to reach the lost or the unchurched. Instead, their purpose is to provide fellowship and encouragement for Christians. These groups may emphasize Bible study and/or prayer. Typically, the group members have met for some time. They may study topics of special interest to the group, but they tend to focus on maturing as believers. Some fellowship groups are for women; others are for men. Most, however, are for couples or coed groups of unmarried adults.

Support Groups

Many churches have established small groups that provide emotional support for troubled persons. Many of these groups are twelve-step groups that aid people with substance abuse problems or eating disorders. Other groups help people who have experienced the loss of a loved one or divorce. There are groups for single parents and grandparents who are raising their grandchildren. Other groups minister to those with all types of addictions. Individuals who suffered abusive childhoods can find a group to help them. Truly, the variety of support groups is remarkable. One pastor joked that his church even had a support group for people who were burned out on support groups.

Seriously, support groups meet many needs, and they are a good way to make contact with unchurched persons in your community. A church in Louisville established a Bible study/support group for single mothers and enlisted seventeen unchurched women in two weeks just by advertising the group on the church's sign.

Evangelistic Bible Studies

Evangelistic Bible studies are an effective means of evangelism. The evangelistic Bible study is the primary evangelistic method used in many mission fields. Often these Bible study groups meet in a home, and they become the means by which whole families are evangelized. The purpose of these Bible studies is to lead people to faith in Christ. Typically, these groups study John's Gospel or other biblical passages suitable for evangelism. Evangelistic Bible studies may serve as the first step in planting a new church, or they may serve as a means of winning people to Christ and channeling them into an established church. Ministries to university students also seek to establish Bible study groups in dormitories in order to do evangelism and follow-up.

EVANGELISM THROUGH SMALL GROUPS

Small-Group Evangelism

Small groups can serve as a tremendous tool in local church evangelism. However, you must take care that the groups are intentionally evangelistic. Charles Arn says that 25 percent of a church's small groups should make evangelism their primary purpose. This requires churches to continually start new groups. Half of all groups stop growing after one year, and almost all stop growing after two years. As the participants in a Bible study group accept Christ, the group transitions to a follow-up group. This is fine and good, but it means that you need to start another evangelism group to take its place.[9]

How can you start new evangelistic groups in your church? George Hunter has listed nine simple steps:

1. Define the target group of people you intend to reach.

2. Research the people in the target group and determine the type of ministry that will meet their needs.

3. Find a committed layperson who will start and lead the group. This person should be similar to and be able to identify with the members of the target group.

4. Train this person to start and lead the group.

5. Begin the recruiting process for members before the group's first meeting.

6. Find an appropriate place to meet.

7. Stress the importance of the first several months.

8. Keep accurate records of the experience for future reference.

9. Build monitoring and evaluation procedures into the program for the first nine months.[10]

To Hunter's list I would add these suggestions:

• Enlist an assistant leader. By enlisting and training leaders you are multiplying the number of leaders.

• Make sure the group meets regularly. Nothing will kill a group faster than inconsistency. If the leader is sick, ask the assistant to conduct the session.

• Divide the group once it grows too large.

• Help the leader find appropriate materials.

Cell-Group Evangelism

Members of cell groups win people to Christ through personal witnessing and evangelistic Bible studies. They also "love" people to Christ. Pastor Yonggi Cho says that each of his church's fifty thousand cell groups loves two people to Christ each year. They notice someone who is not a Christian, and they pray for and serve that person. They prepare special food, assist the person with daily tasks, and do whatever it takes to show they care. When the person asks, "Why are you doing this?" they reply, "Jesus told us to do good to all people, and we want you to know that we love you and Jesus loves you." After two or three months of this, the person accepts Christ and becomes part of the cell group. Thus the person is both saved and congregationalized.[11]

As with small groups, the key to growth through cell groups is to start new cell groups. This comes primarily by dividing existing groups. The term "splitting" sounds negative, so it is better to speak of "dividing" the cell or "birthing" a new group. Group leaders must constantly point toward multiplication, especially since group members tend to cling to the group and are reluctant to divide. Leaders need to constantly remind the group of its evangelistic purpose. The group's focus must remain external, not internal. They also need to remind the members that newcomers are more willing to join a new group than an existing one. Of course, the old and new cell groups can still meet together periodically for fellowship.

EVANGELISM THROUGH THE SUNDAY SCHOOL

Not all Sunday schools are evangelistic, but the Sunday school can be a very effective tool for evangelism. A recent survey of growing Southern Baptist churches found that 60 percent of the leaders said Sunday school was a key part of their outreach. They said, "The problem with nonevangelistic Sunday schools is not the Sunday school program itself, but the failure to utilize the program as an intentional evangelistic tool."[12]

Andy Anderson, a Sunday school growth consultant, teaches that Sunday school yields nine times as many baptisms per decision for Christ as mass evangelism. He notes that typically only one of nine people who make decisions during a mass evangelism event is baptized, while 90 percent of those who profess faith through the Sunday school are baptized. Southern Baptists have found that 50 percent of lost youth and adults enrolled in Sunday school will eventually accept Christ and be baptized.[13]

Flake's Formula for Sunday School Growth

An important factor in the success of Southern Baptist Sunday schools has been Flake's formula. Arthur Flake was a traveling salesman and Sunday school director in a local church. He made a study of effective Sunday schools and began to employ five principles in his own church. Soon other churches asked him to share the principles with them. Eventually, the Baptist Sunday School Board hired him as a field worker. He explained his principles in a book entitled *Building a Standard Sunday School* (1925). Here are his five principles:

1. *Discover the Prospects.* Flake insisted that the first step in outreach is to discover the church's prospects by knowing their names, ages, addresses, and needs. Thus, the first step is to develop a good prospect file.

2. *Expand the Organization.* The second step in growing a Sunday school is to create new classes and departments. The average Sunday school class stops growing after eighteen months. If you want your Sunday school to grow, you must regularly start new classes. By analyzing your present organization and prospects you can determine what classes to begin. A small

church, for example, that has young people in grades 7–12 meeting together would do well to create a new class for junior high students. Calvary Baptist Church in Danville, Kentucky, discovered a need among students at the Kentucky State School for the Deaf. Responding to the need, a class for hearing-impaired persons was created, and eventually a deaf congregation was founded. A church in Dallas saw the need to reach young married couples, so a new couples class was formed and soon had ten couples enrolled.

3. *Train the Workers.* New classes require effectively trained teachers and workers. Growing churches maintain good training programs. Too many churches hand a new teacher a quarterly, and say, "Go teach." It is no wonder that there is so much turnover in teachers. Incompetent teachers repel visitors; excellent teachers attract them.

4. *Provide the Space.* New classes must have somewhere to meet. When most pastors think of adding space, they think of a new building. However, high cost and aggravation should make new building projects a last resort. If you have dual Sunday schools, you can double your space at no cost. Also, a careful space analysis may reveal unused or underused space in your building. Another possibility is to encourage classes to meet somewhere other than the church. For example, one church encouraged a singles class to meet at a local restaurant, so the class meets there for breakfast and Bible study. This arrangement has proved popular and has increased attendance. Another option always available is to have classes meet in members' homes.

5. *Go after the People.* Classes don't reach people; people reach people. Arthur Flake emphasized the importance of visiting prospects. Sunday school teachers and workers need to see outreach as an essential part of their task.

Lewis's Addendum

In his book, *Organize to Evangelize,* Larry Lewis has added three modern principles to Flake's proven formula:

1. *The Principle of Quality Programming.* A strong visitation program is great, but visitors will return only if you provide quality Bible teaching, worship, preaching, and music.

2. *The Principle of Effective Promotion.* In order to reach people you must employ good public relations and effective advertising. Special events and programs can also attract people to your church. People can't come to a church unless they know it exists and where it is located.

3. *The Prayer Principle.* We must never forget that evangelism is God's work and must be done in God's power. If we become mechanistic, relying on methods instead of God, then all our efforts are doomed to failure. We must bathe everything we do in prayer.[14]

You may wonder if Flake's formula still works. I have interviewed a number of pastors, and they say it still works. I had one such interview with Don Mathis, who served as pastor of Central Baptist Church in Corbin, Kentucky, for about ten years. During that time, the church's attendance grew from three hundred to one thousand. When I asked Mathis what methods were used, he said, "We just take Flake's formula and work it to death."

Sunday School Growth Strategies

Kirk Hadaway found a strong relationship between Sunday school and church growth. He reported that 84 percent of growing Southern Baptist churches rated their Sunday schools as excellent or good and that the Sunday school is an effective method for moving stagnant churches off their plateaus.[15] Here are some ways to grow an effective Sunday school.

Enrollment is a key factor. Most Sunday schools report average attendance of 45 to 55 percent of enrollment. That means a Sunday school with enrollment of two hundred will average one hundred in weekly attendance. The way to increase Sunday school attendance is to enroll more people in Bible study. An enrollment campaign can boost your attendance. The Baptist Sunday School Board has developed the "Action Plan" to assist churches in conducting such a campaign. Please note, however, that simply enrolling people in Sunday school is not enough. You will have to visit them and involve them in the class in order to keep them coming.

Start new classes. I've mentioned this principle before but it bears repeating. Growth comes from new classes. A class of elderly men that has been together for forty years is not going to grow, but a new class for single young adults has good potential for growth. Some advocate splitting or dividing classes. You need to be careful about splitting adult classes because your church could end up being split by angry members. It is usually possible to divide classes of children, youth, and young adults, but don't try to divide classes of older folks who have been together for years. I would encourage the creation of new classes much more than the division of existing classes, except with children and youth.

High attendance days are another proven method for increasing Sunday school attendance. Many churches schedule a high attendance day in October or on Easter Sunday. They encourage their teachers and workers to make special efforts at enrollment and visitation before the day. It is best to let the classes or departments set their own goal for this day. If they set it themselves, they will "own" the goal and work harder to accomplish it.

Many evangelistic churches offer an "auditorium class," that is, a large class that meets in the church auditorium and is usually taught by the pastor. This class provides some anonymity for those who may be timid about going into a regular class. It typically covers an evangelistic lesson or a lesson on the basics of Christianity. Churches that have such classes usually try to move the attenders into regular classes after a while.

SUMMARY

Small groups are important because they provide people with a sense of belonging. Relationships are essential to attracting and retaining church members, and small groups provide an ideal setting for the development of personal relationships. Thus, small groups are an effective outreach tool. Churches must continually start new groups because members of these groups tend to cling to each other and seal out newcomers.

Small groups come in all shapes and sizes: Sunday school classes, cell groups, support groups, fellowship groups, and evangelistic Bible studies. All of these have their place. In fact, a larger church might sponsor all of these small groups. To be effective in evangelism the groups must be extroverted and intentionally evangelistic.

Some have written off the Sunday school, but it remains a primary outreach tool for many traditional churches. The key to Sunday school growth is found in following Flake's formula and starting new classes. If you forget everything else, remember this: New growth comes from new units.

STUDY QUESTIONS

1. Why are small groups important to church growth?
2. What are the different types of small groups?
3. What are the advantages of a cell group?
4. What are the principles of Sunday school growth taught by Arthur Flake?
5. What are the advantages of Sunday school over cell groups?
6. What are three methods that can be used for Sunday school growth?

FOR FURTHER STUDY

Anderson, Andy. *Effective Methods of Church Growth: Growing the Church by Growing the Sunday School.* Nashville: Broadman Press, 1985.

George, Carl F. *Prepare Your Church for the Future.* Grand Rapids: Fleming H. Revell, 1991.

Hemphill, Ken and Wayne Jones. *Growing an Evangelistic Sunday School.* Nashville: Broadman Press, 1989.

Lewis, Larry L. *Organize to Evangelize.* Nashville: Broadman Press, 1988.

Neighbour, Ralph Jr. *Where Do We Go from Here? A Guidebook for the Cell Group Church.* Houston: Touch Publications, 1990.

CHAPTER 8

DISCOVER YOUR PROSPECTS

⇒ ———————— ⇐

Your church cannot grow without prospects. Arthur Flake emphasized this and made it the first point in his formula for Sunday school growth. Larry Lewis declares, "Discovering prospects may be the number-one task in any church's outreach for the unreached."[1] If you have a number of good prospects for outreach and evangelism, your church has good potential for growth. If you don't, your potential is poor. In this chapter you will learn some ways to discover prospects. You will have to try various methods in order to find what works best in your community. The important thing is to use some method.

WHY DISCOVER PROSPECTS?

A number of good things happen when a church diligently searches for prospects.

1. *Discover prospects to identify unchurched people.* As you go through your community, you will find lots of people who need to be enrolled in Sunday school or small groups. Many of these people are already Christians, but they are not active in any church. Perhaps they have recently moved to your area or they may have dropped out of another church. Whatever their reason for not being actively involved in a church, they need to participate in Bible study and worship. Children, in many

neighborhoods, would be happy to go to Sunday school if someone would take them. Finding and reaching these children is a blessing indeed—for them and for the church.

2. *Discover prospects to find the lost.* There are lost people in every community, many of whom have no understanding of how to be saved. Some will welcome a witness; others will not. You can't control their response, but you can share the message of salvation with them. Then you will have done your part.

3. *Discover prospects to show your members what needs to be done.* The prospect search may motivate church members to become involved in evangelism and outreach. Church members will often say there are no unchurched or unsaved people in the neighborhood. However, when a survey is completed, they are amazed to see how many prospects there are. The reason for this ignorance is that long-time Christians are friends primarily with other Christians. They may not know new residents unless they are close neighbors. For example, members of rural churches commonly believe there are no prospects in their communities. However, Kevin Ruffcorn states that 40 percent of the people in the average rural community are unchurched.[2] If this is true of rural communities, what must the figure be for urban areas?

4. *Discover prospects to discover ministry needs.* As you visit the homes in your area, you will find many people with social and emotional needs. When you discover these needs, you will be able to help those in difficulty by ministering to them directly and/or referring them to appropriate agencies. Either way, you have met a need in Jesus' name.

5. *Discover prospects to communicate your church's concern.* One summer, two of my students worked from door-to-door doing surveys in the Detroit area. They reported that many people said they were pleased that a church cared enough to inquire about their spiritual welfare. By researching your community, you tell people that God and your church cares for them.

6. *Discover prospects to facilitate your visitation program.* Without an up-to-date prospect file or list, visitation is ineffective. A good visitation program begins with a well-maintained prospect file.

How to Discover Prospects

I have a list of a hundred ways to discover prospects, but I won't discuss all these (surely you're grateful). I will mention only the most important. You will find that some methods work better in your community than others do. Also, you need to use more than one method because you will discover that some folks respond to one approach while others respond to a different approach. The main thing is to identify and locate the unchurched and unsaved.

Friends and Relatives

Church growth research consistently shows that most people join a church because they are related to someone in the church. The same holds true in evangelism. Your best prospects are the friends and relatives of your church members. George Hunter insists that one of the most successful strategies for reaching people is to use existing social networks. Following Donald McGavran, Hunter calls these people "the bridges of God." McGavran and Hunter mean that each person is the bridge to reaching a whole web of people. If you win Barbara to Christ, Barbara then becomes a bridge to reaching her husband, children, parents, siblings, aunts, uncles, cousins, neighbors, coworkers, and other friends.[3]

Larry Gilbert also emphasizes this phenomenon in his book, *Team Evangelism*. He states that 86 percent of the people attracted to a church come because of personal contact with a church member. Many of your church members are not active witnesses for Christ, but all your church members have friends, relatives, and coworkers. Every member can invite these folks to church activities and list them as prospects for you.

Many churches conduct a Friend Day. On this special day, everyone invites a friend to church. New Life Presbyterian Church in Frenchtown, New Jersey, had an average church attendance of 50 people. On Friend Day the attendance registered 154, and two months later the average attendance had increased to 75, a 50 percent increase.[4]

Other churches have an annual Whodo Sunday. On this special day, all members receive cards that read, "Who do you know that would be a prospect for our Sunday school?"

Figure 8.1

WHODO CARD

Who do you know that would be a prospect for our Sunday School?

Name _____

Address_____ Phone_____

Mailing Address (if different) _____

Date of Birth _____ School Grade _____

Please check with me if you need additional information.

_____   _____
Name of Person Giving Information   Phone

The people mentioned on the cards become prime prospects for evangelistic or Sunday school visitation. The use of this card is a good way to begin or update a prospect file.

The In-house Survey is yet another way to discover prospects related to active members. To make an in-house survey, you will need a copy of your church membership roll and your Sunday school roll. Study the rolls to discover relatives of church members who are not participating in worship and Sunday school. When you make the survey, for example, you will discover that you have children in your Sunday school whose parents don't participate. You'll also find that you have active women attending whose husbands don't come with them.

Guests in Worship and Sunday School

Visitors in Sunday school and worship are also excellent prospects. You will want to train your ushers and Sunday school record keepers to be sure to get their names, addresses, and telephone numbers. Many churches now purchase worship folders (bulletins) with detachable guest information forms. Other churches pass out visitors' cards, while others simply place the cards in the pew racks and encourage their guests to fill them out. Be sure to take good care of these cards because you will want to call on these folks as soon as possible.

Parents of Vacation Bible School Children

The parents and siblings of children who attend Vacation Bible School are prospects for your church. Some leaders look at Vacation Bible School merely as an effort of religious education. Surely it is that; however, Vacation Bible School can also provide you with good prospects. The key is information about the families of the children who attend the school. You should visit these family members and list them as prospects for the appropriate Sunday school class or department. Rather than looking on the children as cookie eaters and Kool-Aid drinkers, see them as bridges to reaching whole families for Christ.

New Residents

New residents in your community represent good prospects for your church. When people move from one place to another, they are more open to change in their lives. They will be more open to joining a new church or committing their lives to Christ. Therefore, it is important for you to identify and visit new residents in your community. How can you discover them? You can secure this information in several ways:

- Some towns have a Welcome Wagon that visits all new residents, from which you can request the list of new residents.
- Some utility companies will give you information about new hookups.
- Some newspapers report real estate transactions.
- Many towns have services that supply newcomer information to local businesses for a fee.

Your church members are also excellent sources of information. If you train them, they can serve as your eyes and ears in the community. For example, if one of your members is the secretary at the local elementary school, she could alert you to new residents who have young children. All your church members can watch for new residents in their neighborhoods. Members who work in service businesses will naturally come into contact with folks who identify themselves as new residents. Place prospect cards all over the church building so that people can report these prospects. Even better, encourage them to call the church office with the information. You will need to remind your members about this regularly, but the effort is worthwhile. Their assistance is invaluable. The best advertising is word-of-mouth advertising. If your people stay on the outlook for new residents and speak enthusiastically about their church, that is pure gold!

Many churches automatically mail new residents literature about their church. Churches that offer Wednesday night meals include free tickets. These are good actions, but they are no substitute for personal visitation. When our family moved to Louisville in 1993, we received letters from several Louisville churches even before we left our previous home. When we arrived in Louisville, we also received two visits from Beechwood Baptist Church, the church nearest our home. I was impressed with their efficiency and told them so.

The Door-to-Door Survey

The home survey (sometimes called a religious census) is a tried-and-proven means of discovering prospects. Your church will identify an area and survey every house or apartment in the targeted area. This may be one neighborhood or a whole town. Considering the mobility of American society today, you should plan to survey your community every four or five years. Or, you may want to survey one-fourth of your community every year.

How is a survey conducted? To prepare for a survey, you will need to do these things:

- *Secure a permit.* Some communities have ordinances about doing door-to-door surveys. You will need to check on your community's laws. Get a permit if it is required.

- *Order materials.* You will need to order census cards or survey forms. Be sure to buy enough for every home. It is also advisable to order name/identification tags for the church members who will be doing the survey. The tags reassure people of the workers' purpose.

- *Recruit workers.* Both young people and adults can conduct surveys. The pastor and staff will also need to participate in order to set a good example. You may need also to personally enlist people to work; a general call for volunteers may not produce enough results.

- *Schedule the survey.* You will need to carefully select the date(s) for the survey. Avoid significant school and community events. Also, dates in the fall and spring may offer better weather. Saturday is the best day to survey because more workers are available and because you will find more people at home.

- *Prepare maps.* The survey teams (send them out in pairs) will need clear directions when they are sent out. You don't want to miss any homes, and you don't want to duplicate your efforts. Give each team a marked map so the workers will know exactly where to survey.

- *Provide child care.* You may be able to recruit young adults to help with the survey if you provide child care.

- *Prepare a meal.* Prepare coffee and rolls for the workers when they come in on Saturday morning and prepare a light lunch for them when they come back to report at noon.

When the day of the survey arrives, here are the steps to follow:

- *Welcome the workers.* Thank the workers and serve them coffee, juice, and rolls.

- *Divide the workers into pairs.* Sending the workers out in pairs affords them some protection and makes them feel more secure.

- *Give the workers their assignments.* Distribute the maps you have prepared to the workers. Make certain that the workers understand where they are to go.

- *Instruct the workers.* Tell the workers to go to every home and to fill out the forms completely and legibly. It is better if the workers print the information; sometimes cursive writing is hard to read. If no one is home, they should note that for a return visit. Tell the workers to be friendly but to keep moving. They should be sure to get the ages of children. If someone refuses to answer, ask the workers to write "Refused Information" on the form.

- *Pray for the workers.* Before the workers leave, pray for their warm reception and the success of their labors.

- *Send the workers out.*
- *Collect the forms and file them* carefully when the workers return. Study the forms carefully to discover prospects for your church and opportunities for ministry.

Telephone Surveys

Telephone surveys are growing in popularity. There are several approaches to this method, but "This Phone's for You" may be the best known. Many new churches have used systematic telephone surveys to inform residents of their new church and to discover prospects. Telephone surveys are done by enlisting volunteers who call every residential telephone in a given area. The workers read or recite a prepared message and ask the respondents certain questions. There are certain advantages to this approach:

- It is easier to recruit volunteers for the telephone survey than a door-to-door survey.
- The workers are not at the mercy of the weather.
- The telephone survey goes quickly.
- Some people, especially the elderly, are reluctant to come to the door and speak to strangers.
- In some apartment complexes it is impossible to go door-to-door.

The disadvantages are:

- The telephone survey is less personal than a door-to-door survey.
- Some people find telephone surveys annoying. Telephone solicitors always seem to call me at meal time.

Ministries

The ministries and programs your church offers are all sources of prospects. For example, if your church has a day-care center, a mother's day out, or a kindergarten, all the families involved in these programs could be prospects.

Scripture Distribution

Many churches have successfully used Scripture distribution as a means of finding prospects. It works like this. A church orders copies of the New Testament, preferably in a modern translation. Inexpensive New Testaments that contain the plan of salvation and other helpful information are available. Volunteers deliver the New Testaments to every home in a given area. The volunteers ask where the residents attend church. If the people are unchurched, they become prospects for visitation.

Church Programs

Many growing churches plan special programs and pageants to attract visitors. These are often performed at Christmas and Easter as musicals or dramatic presentations or perhaps as a combination of the two. Some churches have a "Living Christmas Tree" or Passion Play. The keys to the success of these programs are excellent presentations, good advertising, and the careful registration of guests. In order to attract guests, at least for more than one time, the church will have to present an excellent program that will impress visitors. Advertising is important because people can't attend a program they don't know about. Some churches limit admission to those who have tickets, and their members distribute tickets to those who are prospects for the church. When the unchurched attend the program, the church must find some way to ascertain their names and addresses. One way to do this is to ask everyone who attends to fill out a form. The forms of church members can be separated from those of guests.

Community Penetration

In his book *Total Church Life*, Darrell Robinson advocates a plan he calls "Total Penetration." According to his plan, each pastor pinpoints his church on a map. Then the pastor estimates the church's circle of influence. The circle extends as far as the majority of church members live. Once the church's circle of influence is determined, the church will make plans to witness to everyone who lives within the circle. The first stage of witnessing will include general visits and mailouts about special church programs. Once a relationship has been established, members of the church will share the gospel with everyone in the circle of influence. Ideally, the church members will begin with the homes closest to the church and then work their way out. By following this plan, a church can be sure that everyone in the surrounding community has heard the gospel.[5]

Direct Mail

Some churches find prospects by using direct mail. They mail information about their church to all the residences in a given area.

Included in the material is a response card that can be mailed to the church if someone is interested in learning more about it. The success of direct mailings varies greatly. Some churches report little response and feel this method is ineffective. Others, particularly new churches in urban areas, report better results. It is important to get professional help in designing the material to be mailed. Again, excellence is important.

The Action Plan

Andy Anderson developed the "Action Plan" for Sunday school growth. Anderson noted the connection between Sunday school enrollment, Sunday school attendance, and evangelism. Average Sunday school attendance in most churches is 45 to 55 percent of the Sunday school enrollment. For example, if two hundred students are enrolled in Sunday school, the average attendance will be about one hundred. Anderson also noted that people involved in Bible study are much more likely to make a decision for Christ than those who only receive a witness in their homes. Therefore, he concluded that increasing Sunday school enrollment would not only help the Sunday school grow; it would also help the church win more people to Christ.

The "Action Plan" involves the enrollment of anyone who will agree to become a member of a Sunday school class. The members of the classes then visit the new members to get them involved in regular Bible study. The pastor, Sunday School director, teachers, and others carry enrollment cards with them at all times. They enroll people anywhere and everywhere. Many churches have experienced significant growth using this simple approach.

Prospects

Here is Rick Warren's top ten list of prospects:

1. Second-time visitors to your church
2. Close friends and relatives of church members
3. People going through a divorce
4. Those who feel the need for a recovery program
5. First-time parents
6. Those suffering terminal illnesses
7. A couple with major marital problems
8. Parents with problem children

9. Recently unemployed persons or those with financial problems

10. New residents in the community.[6]

Ensure a Pleasant Experience for the Visitors

It takes much effort and many contacts to attract a visitor to church, Sunday school, or a small group. Once you get them to visit your church, it is essential that you make them feel welcome. If you want them to return, you will have to make every effort to see that they have a pleasant experience. Here are some ways to do that:

- Make name tags for everyone in the class or small group.

- Post trained greeters at every entrance.

- Develop a buddy system so that a greeter stays with the guest and escorts him to class or worship and makes introductions.

- Have the class/group members stand and mingle before the study session begins; this will make newcomers feel less conspicuous.

- Make sure that visitors in Sunday school are invited to worship and assign someone from their class to sit with them.

- Encourage your members to invite guests to lunch.

- Bring information about the church to their home (after their visit) along with flowers or a homemade treat.

- Introduce the guests to the pastor and other church leaders.

- Invite guests to a simple reception after church and offer refreshments.[7]

Adopting these suggestions is not a guarantee that your guests will return, but it will demonstrate your openness and concern for them.

SUMMARY

Discovering prospects is a key factor in church growth and evangelism. Searching for prospects not only helps your church reach people; it also communicates your concern to the community. There are many ways to discover prospects. The most likely prospects are people who have some relationship with your church members. New residents and guests in your services are also excellent prospects.

STUDY QUESTIONS

1. Why it is important to discover prospects? Give three reasons.

2. Why are the friends and relatives of your church members the best prospects?

3. What are three ways to discover new residents in your own community?

4. What are the benefits of doing a door-to-door survey?

5. Why do some churches prefer telephone surveys over door-to-door surveys?

FOR FURTHER STUDY

Anderson, Andy. *Effective Methods of Church Growth.* Nashville: Broadman Press, 1985.

Berkley, James D., ed. *Leadership Handbooks of Practical Theology:* vol. 2, *Outreach and Care.* Grand Rapids: Baker Book House, 1994.

Lewis, Larry L. *Organize to Evangelize.* Nashville: Broadman Press, 1988.

Robinson, Darrell W. *Total Church Life.* Nashville: Broadman Press, 1993.

VISIT YOUR PROSPECTS

Most churches suffer from the "Y'all Come Syndrome." They open their doors, shout, "Y'all come," expecting the people of their communities to come to church just because the doors are open, and services are being conducted. But few heed their call. Thousands of these same churches win no one to Christ in a given year. The lost live all around them, but the church members don't go out into the "streets and alleys" of their towns to find them and bring them to Christ (Luke 14:21). If you want your church to become effective in evangelism, you will need to develop an effective visitation program.

WHAT IS VISITATION?

You may think that the term *visitation* is so common that there is no need to define it. However, common words are often misunderstood, and sometimes they are hard to define. Ronald Brown defines *visitation* in this way:

> A direct encounter by an individual with another person for the purpose of understanding and addressing the person's needs, offering encouragement and assistance in the name of Jesus, and declaring through word and/or deed the abiding love and care of God.[1]

Church visitation should be personal, intentional, organized, and purposeful.

Visitation is by nature *personal.* The immediate purpose of visitation is to converse with a person or an entire family. This can be done by one church member or more. The visit can also be done by telephone or E-mail, but it is normally a face-to-face meeting.

Church-related visitation is *intentional.* Church members may come into contact with many people in their daily lives, and it is important to train them to seize these opportunities for outreach and evangelism. However, visitation is intentional, not casual.

When churches conduct visitation, the visits are *purposeful;* that is, the visitors go out with a particular purpose in mind. They may try to enlist new members for a Sunday school class or they might seek to witness to the lost. Whatever the reason, there is a definite purpose for each visit.

Finally, church visitation is organized. Some pastors just encourage all their members to say a word for the church day by day. There is nothing wrong with that as far as it goes. However, "everyone's business is no one's business." Pastors who use that approach will soon find that their churches have plateaued or declined. The only way to ensure that prospects are visited is to organize a program to accomplish that. Larry Lewis insists: "Organized visitation is a must. If people are simply left to their own to visit at their convenience, little will be done."[2]

WHY SHOULD YOU VISIT PROSPECTS?

Churches should visit actively because *Jesus commanded it.* He instructed his followers to "go and make disciples of all nations" (Matt. 28:19). Jesus told a parable that illustrated the need for outreach (Luke 14:15–24). In the parable, the banquet host dispatched his servants first to the streets of the town and then to the country roads to bring people to the banquet. This parable speaks of the kingdom of God. God wants to fill the heavenly banquet hall. That will be accomplished as God's servants today leave the church and go into the streets. Once I was invited to preach at a church in the Philippines. When I arrived, the pastor apologized to me saying, "Brother Mark, I'm sorry there aren't many people here today. Many of our members are out in the villages preaching and teaching." Of course, I assured the pastor that I was thrilled, not offended.

Jesus practiced what he preached. Jesus sent his twelve disciples out two-by-two to visit the towns and villages of Galilee (Matt. 10). Later, Jesus sent out seventy-two of his followers to witness (Luke 10). If we would be like Jesus, we must train and send our members out into the world. Sometimes church walls function like prison walls: they keep the Christians inside and the lost outside.

Churches should visit because they are *loving*. Visitation certainly helps churches, but it primarily helps people. People need to experience new life in Christ and the warmth of church fellowship. They also need the comfort and care that church visitors can provide. Some folks can't come to the church to receive these blessings, and other folks won't come. This should not deter the members of the congregation. If people won't come to them, then they will go to the people. Jesus set a good example for his followers today by traveling all over Palestine to preach, teach, and care for his people.

An effective visitation program is *necessary* for churches to become effective in evangelism. Some churches will grow without an organized visitation program, but these are usually churches located in growing suburbs. They attract new residents with young families. They increase their membership through transfer and biological growth. Also, I know of two megachurches that have grown without a visitation program. Both of these churches are located in metropolitan areas, have dynamic preachers, and use small groups aggressively. Much of their growth comes through the outreach done by and through their small groups. Churches that do not enjoy these advantages will need to develop an effective visitation program.

Most books on church growth emphasize outreach visitation. Kennon Callahan devotes a whole chapter in his popular book, *Twelve Keys to an Effective Church,* to visitation. He says there is a "direct correlation" between visitation and church growth. Lyle Schaller describes visitation as "the second most effective single approach to evangelism today." William Hinson says, "The church that depends on 'walk in' prospects for membership growth will steadily decline. Real growth requires intentional cultivation." Paul Powell explained the growth of his church, Green Acres Baptist

Church in Tyler, Texas, as the result of visitation: "People don't just walk into our church. . . . They come because we first go out to visit them."[3]

Kirk Hadaway conducted a survey of Southern Baptist churches to discover what made them grow. He found that 76 percent of growing churches carry on a weekly visitation program and concluded that "the vast majority of growing churches use visitation as a source of growth. It is a characteristic which tends to separate growing churches from churches which are not growing."[4]

It seems clear, then, that most churches must develop and conduct an aggressive visitation program in order to reach their communities for Christ. The next section tells how to develop and conduct a visitation program.

WHO SHOULD YOU VISIT?

Before you can design an effective visitation program, you must determine whom you are going to visit. Of course, this will vary from place to place. A rural church might have few newcomers to visit but many shut-ins. A suburban church might have many new residents to contact but few members in nursing homes. You will need to study your situation carefully in order to design your visitation program.

I hope you will also decide to take a wholistic approach to visitation. Some pastors see it only as an outreach/evangelistic program, while others view it as a program of pastoral care. It is better to see visitation as both, recognizing that some members will be more gifted in one type of visitation than another. Let the people do what they are willing to do, and take into account their varied spiritual gifts.

What are the different categories of people who need to be visited? Pastor Christopher Jay Johnson studied this issue and developed the following list.[5]

Guest Visitation

You should visit the guests who attend your church's worship services. Some guests are from another place and simply accompany one of your members. You need only send these guests a letter thanking them for their presence. Guests from your community are another matter entirely. These are the best prospects you have. It is essential that you learn their names, addresses, and telephone numbers. This can be done in several ways. You may ask them to fill out a guest card found in the pew rack, or you may want to use the traditional way and ask them to raise their hands to receive cards from the ushers. This identifies them as visitors for the members sitting nearby, but it may also embarrass the guests.

To avoid embarrassing guests, some churches ask everyone to fill out an attendance form. All attenders identify themselves as members or guests. No one is embarrassed because everyone does it. This method also allows the church to track the attendance of members. Most attendance forms have a space for members to report pastoral care concerns and prayer requests. Frazier Memorial Methodist Church in Montgomery, Alabama, has used this method for years with great results.

Another way to identify guests is to appoint a chaplain for each section of seats. The chaplain's role is to welcome and befriend visitors. William Hinson uses this method at the First Methodist Church in Houston, Texas. The larger the church, the more important the human touch becomes. As the shampoo commercial reminds us, "You only get one chance to make a first impression."

Sunday School Visitation

This involves the teachers and outreach leaders in Sunday school classes visiting prospects to enlist them in a Bible study class. Of course, small groups can do the same thing. If you can enroll a lost person in Sunday school, you have a 50 percent chance of winning that person to Christ. That is better than any other method I know. Sunday school or small group visitation is a proven method of evangelism and outreach.

Follow-up Visitation

This involves visiting those who have made professions of faith in your services. Chapter 14 gives more information about this type of visitation. The main thing here is to demonstrate concern for those who have made significant decisions at your church.

New Residents Visitation

New residents are important in church growth. Growing churches work hard to find and visit them. New residents are more open to change; therefore, these folks may be open to the gospel or to joining your church during their first weeks in a community.

Your goal should be to visit them as soon as possible after their arrival. The visitors should be prepared to share information about your church and community. If you have a talented baker in your church, you might ask him or her to bake cinnamon rolls or an apple pie. That would surely get the new residents' attention.

Evangelistic Visitation

This is visitation with the aim of winning a person or persons to Christ. It can be done in a number of ways. Some churches select a neighborhood and go door to door. Darrell Robinson advocates this approach in his book, *Total Church Life*. He believes every church should see to it that each person within its sphere of influence hears the gospel.

The *Whodo Day* is another approach (see p. 106). The church builds a prospect file based on friends and relatives of church members. Some churches have a regular Whodo Day. On this Sunday, church members write the names and addresses of lost friends and loved ones on cards. These cards provide the information for the prospect file. Teams of evangelistic visitors then visit these folks and share the gospel with them.

A third approach, which is tried and true, is to conduct a *religious survey* (or census). Normally the survey will turn up people who have no relationship with Christ, and then the evangelism teams can make an appointment to see them.

Elmer Towns and Larry Gilbert emphasize the Law of Seven Touches in their writings. This law states that on the average, a person will make a decision after the church has contacted the person seven times. Very few people make a decision for Christ the first time they hear the plan of salvation. This means that evangelistic visitors need to see witnessing as a process. They should not see a witnessing interview as a now-or-never event. Rather, they should view the conversation as a step toward a decision for Christ. Once you understand this, your definition of a successful evangelistic conversation changes. Most witnesses believe that an interview is successful only if the person prays to accept Christ. I would contend that a successful evangelistic conversation is one that moves a person a step closer to accepting Christ.[6]

The concept of evangelism as a process becomes clearer when you study Figure 9.1.[7]

Figure 9.1

POST-CONVERSION	16.	Becomes Christlike.
	15.	Observes regular personal devotions and prayer.
	14.	Uses his/her spirtual gifts in local church ministry.
	13.	Personal finances are based on biblical stewardship.
	12.	Accepts and is working toward God's design for the family and home.
	11.	Actively shares his/her faith.
	10.	Participates in discipleship training.
	9.	Faithfully participates in church worship, study groups, or Sunday school.
	8.	Publicly acknowledges faith/conversion (in church or among friends).
S	S.	Salvation/conversion experience. Accepts Christ as Savior.
PRE-CONVERSION	7.	Is willing to repent and accept Christ.
	6.	Realizes sin keeps him/her from salvation.
	5.	Recognizes that Christ is the bridge to God and his/her salvation.
	4.	Realizes he/she is a sinner.
	3.	Believes he/she is responsible to God.
	2.	Has faith that there is a Supreme Being.
	1.	Has only a superficial awareness of God.

Don't be surprised if relatively few of your members volunteer for evangelistic visiting. Many Christians are afraid to witness. Evangelistic training programs will help alleviate the fears of some. Whatever program you choose, on-the-job training should be an essential element. Also, give your members time to gain confidence. Allow your members to try less intimidating types of visitation before they tackle evangelistic visitation.

Inactive Member Visitation

This involves visiting members of the church or Sunday school who are no longer active participants. The reasons for their absence will vary widely, but it is essential that the church discover what the problem is. John Savage conducted a survey of church dropouts and discovered that 100 percent of those interviewed said no one from their church had visited them![8] Considering how much time and effort it takes to enlist a new member, it is a shame to let members slip away without any contact from the church.

Hospital Visitation

Laypersons can be trained to visit hospitals and nursing homes. Some of your members will have both a spiritual gift for and an interest in this kind of visitation. If they are willing and able to do hospital and nursing home visits, the pastor, staff, and trained members will be free to do evangelistic and prospect visitation. Those who visit the hospitals should understand that their ministry is not just to the patients. Family members often have special needs as well. One pastor who served in a small town made it his practice to visit every patient in the local hospital every day. He followed up the contacts he made there, and his church doubled its attendance in five years. Of course, this would not be a practical plan in a large city, but you can grasp the possibilities.

Shut-in Visitation

Most churches have homebound senior adults, many of whom have served the church for several years, but now find themselves physically unable to attend. Churches would do well to organize "care teams" to visit these saints and minister to their needs.

Visitation of the Grieving

This category involves visiting those in the church family who are experiencing grief. When we think of this, we immediately think of those who have recently lost a loved one. However, we often forget that grief resurfaces at holidays and other special occasions. Those who do this type visitation will need some training, but their ministry will be greatly appreciated.

HOW SHOULD A VISITATION PROGRAM BE ORGANIZED?

A few churches are able to grow without an organized visitation program, but your church probably won't. If you want your church to reach people for Christ and grow, you will have to organize your members to go out and get them. Organizing a visitation program can be described with ten key words.

Motivation

Most church members would rather stay home than go visiting. Wouldn't you rather sit in your recliner and watch a ball game than go visiting? Well, so would they. If you want church members to visit, you will have to motivate them. Many pastors try to motivate their people with guilt. This works well for a while, but not for long. Only positive motivation works well in the long run.

How can you motivate people to visit without resorting to guilt?

- *Preach and teach evangelism and outreach.* Instill in your people the conviction that evangelism is a primary function of the church.

- *Promote outreach in the announcements, sermon, and church newsletter.* Emphasize the importance of visitation in every way you can. Ask faithful visitation workers to give testimonies about their experiences.

- *Set an example.* They won't do more than you do; if you don't visit, they won't visit either. How many visits should you make each week? Larry Lewis believes a pastor should make at least fifteen outreach/evangelistic visits each week. Kirk Hadaway says five prospect visits per week is a bare minimum to maintain church growth.[9]

- *Invite people to go with you.* Lots of members know they ought to visit, but they are timid. If you ask them to go with you, they will cheerfully go, trusting that you will do the talking. When they have gone with you (or some other experienced worker) several times, they may be prepared to go and take a novice with them.

Organization

The essential element to any organized visitation program is the prospect file. This is some sort of file that contains the names of people who need a visit. As mentioned earlier, these people will fall into several categories. If you use three-by-five-inch cards to record your prospects' names and addresses, you may want to color code the cards. Thus blue cards might represent Sunday school prospects, white cards new residents, yellow cards evangelistic prospects, and so on. These cards can be stored in file boxes with a separate box for each category. The advantage of three-by-five-inch cards is that they fit easily into a shirt pocket or purse.

Another system is one marketed by the Baptist Sunday School Board called the "Prospect Assignment Pocket and Card." This is a system of paper pockets that fit into a three-ring binder. Each pocket has the name, address, telephone number, and age of a prospect. It also indicates which Sunday school class or department has responsibility for the prospect. The pocket remains at the church. Within the pocket there is a card which the worker takes on the visit. The same information about the prospect is written on the top of the card, but the bottom of the card has blank space for reporting visitation results. Many churches have reported using this system satisfactorily.

Some churches use computers to record and trace prospects. They print out lists of prospects every week. The computer can arrange these lists by category, age group, or location. The obvious advantage of this system is the ease with which the prospect file can be maintained.

Use whatever system you like, but use something. Nothing will discourage your visitation workers faster than mistaken assignments. It takes a lot of effort to enlist and motivate visitation workers. If they receive a card with an incorrect address or arrive at an address only to find that their prospect moved six months ago, their morale will plummet, and you will have a hard time getting them to come out again.

How can you avoid problems like these? It is important to recruit and train a visitation secretary. This is someone who will maintain the visitation file. The visitation secretary should update the prospect file weekly. This means adding new cards (for guests who attended last Sunday) and removing cards. Cards should be removed when the person joins your church (or another church), leaves the community, or dies. The secretary and the outreach leader should see to it that the best prospects are visited that week. Naturally, you will want to give priority to those who visited your church recently as well as those with special needs.

You should diligently train your workers to record the results of their visits. For example, if the prospect has a big guard dog, other visitors will appreciate knowing that. Or, if a prospect works nights and sleeps days, that information will help you avoid antagonizing someone. Visitors should also record and report the results of their conversations. For instance, if you visit a family with a newborn baby, the church's preschool director should be notified so that she can visit them. Or, someone may need a special visit from the pastor. Alert visitation workers can serve as the eyes and ears of the congregation.

An army in the field can't function without support troops. The same holds true for your visitation workers. Recruiting some support workers may enable you to send out more workers—providing child care at the church so some mothers can visit, for example. Some churches provide a meal for their visitation workers; someone will have to prepare this. You may also want to recruit prayer warriors who will support the workers in their efforts. You may have folks who will cheerfully perform these adjunct tasks but would never go visiting. Encourage and affirm them in what they are willing to do. Their service may free up someone to visit who has a genuine gift for it. Let people do what they are willing to do.

Finally, it is important to practice *multiple assignment of prospects.* Here is the way Green Acres Baptist Church in Tyler, Texas, does it:

1. On Monday the names of church guests and newcomers to the community are assigned to the pastor or a staff member.

2. These same prospects are assigned to a Sunday school class.

3. The prospects are assigned to a deacon.

4. Prospects are assigned to a church member who lives nearby. The member is encouraged to visit the prospects and take them a cake or pie or flowers.[10]

Paul Powell admits that this multiple assignment of prospects may seem like overkill, but he also vouches for its effectiveness. Remember the Law of Seven Touches.

Leadership

An effective visitation program must have a leader. Most often this is the pastor, who has the responsibility to set an example for the church members to follow. Some larger churches have a staff member direct the program. This is fine, but the pastor must still play a prominent and visible role. Your church may have a layperson who is willing and able to take on this task of leadership. Perhaps a retired person may want to take on this challenge. Also, don't forget to enlist retired pastors and missionaries. Their cooperation will prove invaluable. You may want to assign team leaders who will coordinate each type of visitation. For example, the Sunday school director might coordinate the visitation of prospects for the Sunday school, while a deacon might coordinate the visitation of shut-ins. Finally, remember to enlist and train a visitation secretary. Without proper maintenance of your prospect file, your whole program will come to a grinding halt.

Training

Most types of visitation require some training. For example, those visiting hospitals and nursing homes should receive several hours of training. The same would hold true of those who visit the grieving. Those who make evangelistic visits should be trained to share their personal testimony and give a simple presentation of the plan of salvation. Materials are available for training all types of visitors, but the key element is on-the-job training. New workers can benefit from training classes, but classroom instruction must be reinforced by practical experience. Jesus trained his disciples by observation, imitation, and application. You can't improve on that.

Scheduling

Many churches struggle to find a good time for visitation. You will have to experiment to find what is best in your situation. In my own experience, the time that worked best was Wednesday evening. Our workers would come to church for supper at 5:30; from 6:00 to 7:00 they visited; and then they returned for prayer meeting. I tried many different times, but this seemed to work out the best for most people. Our workers appreciated the fact that they did not have to come out an extra night each week.

You may also want to consider having different types of visitation at different times. For example, you might want to have women's visitation. In some communities, most households are headed by women. Women can visit these single parents more effectively than men. You might want to schedule youth visitation on Saturdays. Older folks don't want to drive at night, but they are willing to visit during the day.

Whatever you do about scheduling, be sure to contact guests in your Sunday service as soon as possible. Herb Miller says, "No other single factor makes a greater difference in improving annual membership additions than an immediate visit to the homes of first-time worshipers." Miller's research produced these startling statistics. If laypeople make fifteen-minute visits to the homes of those who visit the worship service within thirty-six hours, 85 percent return the following week. If the guests are visited within seventy-two hours, the percentage drops to 60 percent, and those visited after one week return at a 15-percent rate. Moreover, if the pastor visits instead of a layperson, this percentage of repeat guests is halved.[11]

Many church visitation workers call and make appointments before they visit a prospect. This cuts down on wasted visits, and it shows common courtesy. This practice is almost a necessity in light of the hectic schedules many people keep these days.

Materials

You will need to anticipate the materials your workers will need. These include maps, brochures about the church, evangelistic tracts, calling cards, and door hangers. Door hangers are card stock advertisements with the church's name, address, and schedule printed on them. They can be hung on the door knob or handle. Usually, they have a space on which to write a message. These door hangers are useful because workers can leave them if they find no one at home. Thus, the trip to the prospect's home is not wasted. Many churches have calling cards printed. These show the church's name, address, and telephone number. Visitors can write their names in the place provided and leave these cards. Finally, wise churches develop attractive brochures. These will draw people to your church. Be sure to have all these materials ready when your workers come to pick up their prospect assignments. You will not want to waste a minute of visitation time.

Encouragement

If you encourage your workers, they are more likely to continue their visitation work. Tell your workers how much you appreciate them. Praise them individually and as a group. Call them on the telephone or write them notes expressing your gratitude.

Evaluation

You will need to constantly monitor and evaluate your visitation program. Years ago I served a church that was very evangelistic. We would go out witnessing every Tuesday night. After a time, we found fewer and fewer people at home. When the pastor changed visitation to Monday night, we found everyone at home. In fact, one man said, "What are you doing here? It's not Tuesday night!"

You will need to monitor both participation and results. Ask for feedback from your workers. Also, read the reports they write on the prospect cards. Go with your workers to assess their effectiveness and the need for further training. If you have visitation team leaders, meet with them periodically to evaluate the program.

Variety

"Variety is the spice of life." That proverb certainly applies to visitation. Visitation programs easily fall into ruts. The same-old-same-old may put your program and church to sleep. What can you do? Try shifting the schedule every so often. During the summer you might have visitation once a month instead of weekly. Before a revival or high attendance Sunday, you might have a visitation blitz. Try distributing New Testaments or magazines to everyone in a neighborhood. The main thing is to make some changes every so often.

Recognition

By recognizing and honoring your visitation workers, you will keep them coming back and more easily recruit new workers. You can recognize workers in many ways. If someone they visited joins the church, ask the worker to stand beside the person at the front of the church. Honor a worker of the week by putting his name and photo in the church paper. Recognize the worker from the pulpit.

Several years ago I attended a revival meeting. That night was an old-fashioned pack-the-pew night. The pastor had appointed a pew captain for each pew. During the service the pastor identified every pew captain by name and bragged on each one shamelessly. He also gave each one an award, and the captain who brought the most received a special prize. I thought the whole thing was corny and old-fashioned until I noticed the expressions on the workers' faces. They loved it! On further inquiry I discovered that the pastor had a well-functioning visitation program and an enthusiastic corps of visitors. He understood the importance of recognition.

Finally, I would suggest that you honor your visitation workers at a banquet or dinner each year. This is a good way to show them how much their faithfulness means to you and to the church.

SUMMARY

Most churches need to organize a visitation program in order to reach people for Christ. Visitation is both biblical and practical. Jesus sent his disciples out witnessing, and you should send your members out as well. Organization and training are the two keys to an effective visitation program. You will need to develop a prospect file and a system for dispatching workers to visit prospects. You can enhance the effectiveness of your workers by training them. On-the-job training will allay their fears and instill confidence. The pastor and staff set the pace for the whole congregation. If they actively visit, the members will follow their example.

STUDY QUESTIONS

1. What is the definition of *visitation?*
2. Why do churches need organized visitation programs?
3. What types of visitation should churches do?
4. Can you list the ten key words in visitation organization?

FOR FURTHER STUDY

Callahan, Kennon L. *Twelve Keys to an Effective Church.* San Francisco: HarperCollins, 1983.
Lewis, Larry L. *Organize to Evangelize.* Nashville: Broadman Press, 1988.
Piland, Harry M. *Going . . . One on One.* Nashville: Convention Press, 1994.

CHAPTER 10

DEVELOP WEEKDAY MINISTRIES

Growing churches establish multiple entry points through which new members can join the congregation. This requires adding more ministries to meet your community's needs. Gary McIntosh and Glen Martin say, "Churches that are effectively reaching people for Christ see the needs of the unchurched, establish ministries that allow the church to be present in the community, and have a process by which they are able to draw these unchurched people into the safety of Christ and a local church."[1]

For many years, successful churches followed this formula: great preaching, wonderful music, and a dynamic Sunday school. When they combined these elements with a beautiful building and an able pastor, success was practically guaranteed. Churches like this still prosper in the South, and they still attract "builders" (the generation born before 1940). However, the younger generations, the boomers and busters, have different expectations. They are looking for churches that will respond to their personal and family needs.[2]

Many established churches are introverted. They devote most of their attention and resources to meeting the needs of their members. More aggressive congregations have become what Lyle Schaller calls "Seven-Day-a-Week Churches." These churches are extroverted churches that provide an array of services and ministries to attract people and meet the needs of their communities.

These full-service churches develop multiple ministries that provide entry points for new people. The ministries and programs enable the churches to make contact with people outside their congregations. The programs also show the community that the church cares about them and their needs. Seven-day-a-week congregations want to reach people for Christ, but they realize that Sunday school classes and Sunday morning worship services may not be sufficient to accomplish their evangelistic purpose.

Seven-day-a-week churches understand that the consumer-oriented boomers and busters shop around for the church that best meets their needs. These churches also understand that some people are not able to participate on Sunday mornings. One person in five works on Sunday; nurses, police officers, fire fighters, waitresses, and many others are often unable to participate in Sunday morning activities. Others may prefer not to participate on some Sundays, but they would attend services at other times. For this reason, many full-service churches offer worship on Saturday nights. Creative churches look for opportunities to reach people seven days a week.[3]

VACATION BIBLE SCHOOL

The Vacation Bible School is probably the best-known and most widely used weekday ministry. Larry Lewis believes, "Greater church growth can be achieved in a shorter time with Bible School than any other means." He notes that one of every three unsaved children will be won to Christ during the school. It is also significant that participants receive as much biblical instruction in a one-week program as they do in three months of Sunday school.[4]

Conducting a VBS is hard work, but it can pay big dividends. The Baptist Sunday School Board reports that typically one-third to one-half of VBS enrollees are not participating in Bible study in any church. In 1993 the Prestonwood Baptist Church had 3,360 people enrolled in VBS. Sixty-five percent of these students were not members of the Sunday school program, and 40 percent were unchurched. In the same year, Fairview Baptist Church, a small church in Mohawk, Tennessee, enrolled 226 pupils. Among these the church discovered forty-two prospects, and eight people made professions of faith. Small wonder then that Willie Beaty, former VBS consultant at the Sunday School Board, says he knows of no other project or event "that will do a better job of putting churches in touch with lost people."[5]

As you plan and conduct your VBS, you will want to keep the following pointers in mind:

Make Your Plans Early

Get started early, and remember four important steps:

- Schedule the dates carefully. Many churches hold VBS in June, about two weeks after the schools have dismissed for summer vacation. If you have VBS right after public schools dismiss, you'll find the children very restless. It's better to wait until they have a couple of weeks to become bored.
- Check on the dates of VBS workshops. These provide good training for workers.
- Set the time for the VBS. Many churches have begun holding VBS at night in order to enlist enough workers.
- Order your teaching materials early. The earlier you put these materials into the hands of your workers, the better.

Promote and Publicize

You'll want to enlist creative and energetic people to serve on the publicity committee. Here are some methods they can use to advertise the VBS:

- A parade
- Direct mail
- Posters
- Flyers/handbills
- Yard signs
- Radio/television ads
- Newspaper ads

It is important to list the church's telephone number on all the advertisements so that people can call for information. You will also want to feature your church's name and address prominently. If you are targeting specific neighborhoods, you may want ask your young people to go door-to-door through the neighborhood distributing handbills.

Enlist and Train Workers

The workers are the key to a successful VBS. Surely there will be a special place in heaven for these faithful workers. Some workers serve year after year, and they may need little training. However, you may be able to enlist some new workers if you assure them that they will receive proper training. Young people can serve effectively as helpers during VBS. You can schedule their Bible study during a later week, and this will free them to help with the children's VBS.

Preenroll the Students

Before the VBS begins, preenroll all the children involved in your Sunday school. This will save time on the first day of VBS.

Keep Good Records

By keeping good records, you will accomplish two things. First, you will be able to gauge the growth of your VBS from one year to another. Second, the records will help you identify prospects for visitation.

Sponsor Special Days

Special days will increase your attendance and excitement. There are lots of things to do: a VBS Olympics, a watermelon feast, a clown show, a puppet show, a tricycle race, a costume day, and bring-a-friend day. Use your creativity, and everyone will have fun.

Visit Each Department

Some pastors leave town during VBS; they do not want to be bothered. I believe these pastors underestimate the importance of this program. VBS week is an opportunity for the pastor to get to know the children, and for the children to get to know their pastor better. I suggest that the pastor visit every department. The pastor may tell a Bible story or answer questions about the church and the work of a pastor. The main thing is to interact with the children. If you come to know unchurched children, then you will have a better possibility of reaching them and their parents.

Conduct a Decision Service

During the week you will want to have a decision service for the older children. I suggest you limit this to children ten years of age and older. Take care not to pressure the children into a premature decision. Instead, explain the plan of salvation simply and ask them to respond if they feel led to do so. Be sure to counsel with those who make decisions. It would be wise to arrange for counselors to be present so they can help you deal with the children who make professions of faith. Encourage the children to share their decision with their parents. Afterwards you will need to visit the children and parents in their homes to clarify the decision and speak to them about baptism.

Schedule Commencement Service at a Convenient Time

You will want to hold a commencement service. This service provides you with an opportunity to bring the children's parents and relatives to the church facilities. If you schedule the time carefully, you can maximize attendance. If you have everyone register, you will acquire a number of prospects.

Assign Prospects for Follow-up

Vacation Bible School can provide you with good prospects. However, your church growth will not be affected by VBS unless someone visits the prospects. Move quickly to assign the prospects to visitation workers so the visits will be made while VBS is still fresh on the prospects' minds. VBS can be a powerful tool for evangelism and growth.

SOCIAL MINISTRIES

Some churches emphasize social ministry. Others emphasize evangelism. Some evangelicals consider evangelism and social ministries to be mutually exclusive. Jesus was among the few who emphasized both evangelism and social ministry. He preached the good news of the Kingdom, but he also healed the sick and fed the hungry. A balanced, biblical ministry cares for the whole person: spiritually, physically, and emotionally. Missionary and evangelist E. Stanley Jones stated: "An individual gospel without a social gospel is a soul without a body, and a social gospel without an individualized gospel is a body without a soul. One is a ghost and the other is a corpse."[6]

A popular term used to describe this wholistic approach to evangelism is *ministry evangelism.* Charles Roesel, pastor of the First Baptist Church of Leesburg, Florida, is one of the best-known proponents and practitioners of this approach. He defines ministry evangelism this way:

> Ministry evangelism is simply caring for persons in the name of Jesus Christ. It is meeting persons at the point of their need and ministering to them physically and spiritually. The intent of ministry evangelism is to present the good news of God's love in order to introduce persons to Jesus. Ministry evangelism is not manipulative. Ministry is

given lovingly and unconditionally. But the reason for it all, God's love for lost persons, is always shared.[7]

Delos Miles, longtime professor of evangelism, believes "that social involvement and evangelism are partners."[8] I certainly agree. Sometimes social ministry prepares the way for evangelism, winning a hearing for the gospel. At other times evangelism comes first, and social ministry follows as new believers live out their faith. Neither is a substitute for the other. Rather, one hand washes the other, and both are better for their partnership.

The First Baptist Church of Leesburg, Florida, provides a good example of a church practicing ministry evangelism. Leesburg is a town of about 25,000 in central Florida. In 1970 the church had 1,398 members and a budget of $100,000. In 1995 the church had grown to 6,000 members, and the annual budget was $2 million. In 1970 the church baptized fewer than 20 persons, while in 1994 the church baptized more than 300 people. What made the difference? In 1982 the church embarked on ministry evangelism by establishing its first social ministry, a rescue mission.[9]

In the past thirteen years the church has developed eighty-two different ministries including the following:

Rescue Mission for Men	Women's Shelter
Teen Home	Furniture Barn
Pregnancy Care Center	Children's Rescue Shelter
Clothing Closet	Food Pantry

More than fourteen hundred volunteers work in the ministries, and the church has constructed a $2 million complex called Ministry Village. The money for the construction was raised without a special building campaign.[10] All of the ministries meet community needs, while maintaining an evangelistic emphasis. Pastor Roesel says, "This is not the old 'social gospel' resurrected; this is ministry evangelism. I exist for evangelism as fire exists for burning. We don't have a single ministry but that the goal is to reach every person involved with the gospel of Jesus Christ."[11]

There are three keys to this dynamic ministry evangelism at Leesburg. First, the pastor preaches and models the ministry; second, the pastor and staff help all the members discover and use their spiritual gifts. They encourage the people to find or develop a ministry in which they can employ their gifts. Third, the pastor and staff continually emphasize the need for evangelism in all their ministries; this is essential because many church social ministries never share a verbal witness of salvation. Elton Trueblood has written: "Testimony must be both deed and word. The spoken word is never really effective unless it is backed up by a life, but it is also true that the living deed is never adequate without the support which the spoken word can provide."[12]

How can you develop social ministries in your community? The first thing to do is to *survey the community*. Surveys should cover both ordinary citizens and community leaders. Through these surveys you can discover special needs that exist in your area. For example, if many immigrants live in your community, you may decide to offer English classes. Or, if many members of your community can't read, you may need to offer literacy classes. Certainly poor people have many needs, but so do white collar workers. The Wilshire Baptist Church in Dallas, Texas, offered a seminar on "The Spirituality of Nursing," and drew 60 nurses the first year. The second year the seminar was offered, the enrollment was 120 and 40 people had to be turned away due to a lack of space. This church also developed a New Teachers Support Group, and 43 teachers participated.[13]

The second thing to do is to *survey the members of your congregation*. This will help you identify their interests, talents, experiences, and spiritual gifts. When you know your congregational resources, you can begin to match resources with needs. For example, a retired elementary teacher might be happy to serve as a literacy teacher. Or, an experienced mechanic might be willing to assist widows and divorced women with car repairs.

The third step is to *pray about the needs*. There are more needs in every community than any single church or group of churches can meet. Which needs should your church address? Ask your people to pray for God's direction. If they feel led to develop certain ministries, their enthusiasm and commitment will certainly be greater than if you decide for them.

The fourth step is to *provide appropriate training*. Some church members may feel led to a certain ministry, but that does not mean they are immediately qualified to participate in that particular ministry. Jesus called his disciples to ministry, but he then spent three years preparing them for it. In your church someone might want to work with persons recovering from substance abuse. That is a worthwhile ministry, but you will want to be sure that a professional counselor trains the member to do it. Good intentions are not enough; members have to learn how to help people in helpful rather than hurtful ways.

The fifth step is to *develop policies and procedures for the ministry.* This process of development will help the workers think through what they plan to do. It will also assist the people who join the ministry later or eventually take it over.

One of the most exciting examples of ministry evangelism is Mission Arlington, a ministry sponsored by the First Baptist Church of Arlington, located between Dallas and Fort Worth, Texas. Tillie Burgin and six hundred volunteers work with more than 150 Bible study groups and house churches that minister to more than two thousand people every week. Tillie and her associates have developed more than fifty different ministries that include medical clinics, dental clinics, a halfway house for released prisoners, a counseling center, and a warehouse full of clothes and food. This church and others have shown that there is no contradiction between social ministry and evangelism.[14]

MINISTRY TO SENIORS

If you read magazines and newspapers, you are probably aware that the number of senior citizens in the United States is rapidly increasing. Some writers call this "The Gray Wave." In 1995 more than thirty million Americans were over the age of sixty-five, and seniors make up an increasing portion of the population. Seniors have special needs that churches need to meet, and they also represent a resource churches can tap.[15]

Senior citizens need to know Christ just as other generations do. Churches can make contact with seniors by providing varied programs especially to senior citizens. These can include support groups that deal with grief and other problems; activity groups that offer fun and fellowship; and, special seminars on health, safety, and financial issues. Churches can also meet the needs of the elderly by providing day care for the infirm, transportation, yard maintenance, home repairs, or referral services to the community and government agencies.

Many churches offer Bible classes, worship services, and other programs at retirement and nursing homes. Before beginning any of these programs, you will need to speak to the administrator(s) and ascertain what is already being done. Some homes are inundated with church groups, while others are neglected. Also be aware that many residents are unable to come to the activity room. Enlist enough volunteers to visit room-to-room. You will find many saints in nursing homes, but you will also find opportunities for evangelism. I once led an eighty-five-year-old woman in a nursing home to Christ.

Many churches are realizing that retired persons are a valuable ministry resource. They have years of experience and the time to put it to good use. You may want to develop a special witnessing training program for seniors. They will have more success in witnessing to older prospects than younger workers will.

RECREATION MINISTRIES

Drive by any public park on a nice day, and you will see lots of folks jogging, roller blading, or playing softball. Recreational activities can provide invaluable entry points for your church and are especially attractive to youth and young adults. I heard of one church that won lots of young men to Christ through its basketball league. Every team had to have at least two lost men on it. When those men were won to Christ, the team had to divide and reorganize with two lost men on each of the two new teams. In this way the church won forty to fifty young men each year.

The example I just cited is the good news. The bad news is that not all recreation programs win people to Christ or attract people to the church. Some even repel people. What are the problems? Some Christians are so competitive that they forget to act like Christians. I have seen bench-clearing brawls at church league softball and basketball games. One umpire told me he would rather work industrial league games than church league games!

Women and seniors also enjoy recreational programs. Many churches offer aerobics classes for women and special exercise programs for seniors. By surveying your congregation and community, you can discover whether there is any interest in these types of programs.

What can you do to ensure that your church does it right? First, define your church's sports philosophy. What do you hope to accomplish through athletic programs? Be sure to clearly communicate this philosophy to all who participate, especially the coaches. Second, screen your coaches carefully. A coach with a "win-at-any-cost" approach will not be an asset, no matter how much the coach knows about the sport. Spiritual maturity and a heart for outreach are more important. Third, establish rules of conduct and enforce them strictly. Finally, make sure that members of your church staff participate if possible, or at least attend some of the games. This participation will enable you to get to know your people better (you may see a side of Joe he doesn't show on Sunday morning), and it will help you relate to prospects.[16]

CHILDREN'S MINISTRIES

One of the best ways to reach families in your community is to minister to their children. All parents are concerned about their children. Meeting their children's needs will endear you to the parents and open doors of communication. Churches can minister to children through a variety of programs, all of which are beneficial in many ways: mothers' day out, kindergarten, day care, after-school programs, day camp, and children's choirs. All of these programs should be nonprofit and designed to meet the needs of families. If your church decides to implement one of these programs, you will need to carefully research to uncover government regulations that apply to facilities and staffing.

The Little Flock Baptist Church in Shepherdsville, Kentucky, has established an Academy of Arts to attract children and youth to the church. The "Academy" offers private and group lessons in music and drama. Not every church has the personnel to offer a program like this, but most churches can at least sponsor children's choirs.

Backyard Bible clubs are another good way to reach children, especially in the summer. These clubs may meet wherever you can find a place. Excellent materials are available, and workers can use them with only a little training.

Summary

Growing churches continually develop new entrance points into their churches. These churches are extroverted churches; they are concerned about the needs of the community, not just the needs of their own members. They survey their communities to discover their needs, and they develop programs to meet those needs. The programs and ministries enable them to meet unchurched people and draw them into the church's sphere of influence.

These extroverted churches can be called seven-day-a-week churches because they sponsor programs throughout the week. These might include Vacation Bible School, recreation programs, seniors activities, mothers' day out, and an after-school program. They are all designed to meet needs and help people find new life in Christ.

Lay leaders are the key to all church programs. Service-oriented churches empower their members by helping them discover their spiritual gifts. Once the members know how they are gifted, they can employ their gifts to build up the church.

Study Questions

1. How is a seven-day-a-week church different from a traditional church?

2. Why does a church need multiple entry points?

3. How does Charles Roesel define "ministry evangelism"?

4. How can Vacation Bible School enhance a church's evangelism program?

5. How can a recreation program help or hurt a church?

6. What are four children's programs that churches can offer?

For Further Study

Atkinson, Donald, and Charles Roesel. *Meeting Needs/Sharing Christ.* Nashville: Convention Press, 1995.

Furness, Charles Y. *The Christian and Social Action.* Old Tappan, N.J.: Fleming H. Revell Co., 1972.

Miles, Delos. *Evangelism and Social Involvement.* Nashville: Broadman Press, 1986.

Pinson, William M. Jr. *Applying the Gospel.* Nashville: Broadman Press, 1975.

Schaller, Lyle. *The Seven-Day-a-Week Church.* Nashville: Abingdon Press, 1992.

CHAPTER 11

REACH PEOPLE
THROUGH WORSHIP

W orship is the front door to the church in the 1990s. Sunday school once filled this role, and it still does in some churches, but most people now make their first contact with the church through worship. William Easum, a Methodist church growth consultant, writes, "The vast majority of people attend worship before any other church activity."[1] Kennon Callahan agrees: "More often unchurched persons find their way first to the service of worship. Thus, corporate worship becomes an increasingly important avenue through which people are reached on behalf of Christ."[2]

The worship service has a clear connection to evangelism and church growth. Most Protestant churches in North America offer a public invitation at the end of the service where they invite people to accept Christ or to unite with the church. If the worship service is not meant to reach people for Christ and his church, why offer a public invitation? Some would argue that worship is only for Christians; however, George Barna's research shows that 50 percent of unchurched Americans are most interested in connecting with a church through the Sunday morning worship service.[3] Hence, evangelistic churches must plan and conduct their worship services with unchurched and unsaved prospects in mind.

143

UNDERSTAND THE NATURE OF WORSHIP

Worship is something we do a lot, but we seldom define it. The English word *worship* comes from an Anglo-Saxon word *weorthscipe,* which means "to ascribe worth." Certainly God deserves our praise because he is worthy. However, this definition is not adequate because it does not describe the full implications of worship. Chevis Horne suggests the following brief definition: "Worship is coming into the presence of Almighty God to offer him adoration and praise."[4]

If you prefer a longer, more formal definition, perhaps you will agree with James Emery White, who defines worship in this way: "Christian worship is the active response of a community of believers to the glory of the living God which properly attributes praise and honor to God for who he is and what he has done while contributing to the growth and development of that community of believers."[5]

Worship must be the primary activity of the church. Theologian W. T. Conner wrote: "The worship of God in Christ should be at the center of all else the church does. It is the mainspring of all the activity of the church. . . . The whole life and organization of the church should spring from worship, center in worship, and end in worship."[6] Thus, effective worship will draw believers into fellowship with God and prompt them to evangelize the lost.

PROVIDE A CONDUCIVE SETTING

Churches that want to reach people through worship give careful attention to the worship setting. The setting includes facilities, conditions, and accessibility. While no church can provide a perfect worship setting, most churches could improve their worship settings considerably.

Facilities

If you want your church to reach people for Christ, you will have to evaluate and improve your facilities. Though they are not an end in themselves (You may need to remind the building and grounds committee of this!), facilities are an asset to use in reaching people.

Signs. Growing churches post good signs that guide visitors to the church and its parking facilities. The visitors' parking area should be clearly marked and conveniently close to the church building.

Signs should also direct guests to the appropriate entrance. Once, when my family and I visited a large urban church, we could not figure out which door to use to enter the building. Finally, we asked an arriving church member for assistance. She guided us to the correct building, but it would have taken us some time to figure it out for ourselves. Signs don't cost much; post a lot of them.

Parking. Growth-oriented churches reserve the best parking spaces for guests and handicapped persons. Adequate parking is basic to church growth. If your parking lot is full, your church's attendance will probably plateau. Check your parking lot regularly to monitor its use. Some churches use parking attendants to make the best use of their parking spaces. Growth-oriented pastors and staff members are willing to sacrifice their reserved parking places for worship guests. Bob Russell, pastor of Southeast Christian Church in Louisville (which averages ten thousand in worship), often jokes about having to park in the "back forty." I'm sure lots of pastors would gladly walk a long distance to preach to such crowds.

Space. Churches concerned about outreach monitor their space, both for worship and education. James Emery White states two important truths in regard to space: "Don't have too little and don't have too much."[7] An auditorium that is too full discourages worship attendance, and an auditorium that is too large dampens enthusiasm. People don't like to feel crowded, but they don't like to feel as if they are rattling around in an empty building. Once, while on vacation in Florida, I visited a church with about one hundred worshipers in an auditorium with a seating capacity of six hundred. The circumstances seemed to shout, "There's something wrong here!"

How do you go about planning for expansion? When a building is 80 percent full, you should plan to expand. Your facilities can expand in several ways. First, you can build a new facility. This is the most common practice, but it is also the most expensive. Another possibility is to offer a second worship service and/or Sunday school. This option allows you to double space at no cost. However, it requires lots of planning, especially if you are starting a second Sunday school because you will need twice as many teachers and workers. A third option is to meet in off-campus facilities. Churches that decide to build new facilities should build just ahead of growth. Many churches overestimate their growth potential and overbuild. Worshiping in a largely empty building may hinder growth, and large debt payments may inhibit church staffing and programming.

Rest rooms. Many people judge an institution by the appearance and cleanliness of its rest rooms. You may need to remodel your rest rooms. Monitor their cleanliness regularly.

Attractiveness. Do everything you can to make your building more attractive. I recently visited a church with good carpeting, beautiful stained-glass windows, and handsome oak pews. However, the visual center of the auditorium, the pulpit area, was ugly. The furniture on the platform did not match and the rail in front of the choir was covered with a faded velvet curtain. Ask an interior decorator for advice. Often a few minor adjustments can greatly enhance a facility's appearance.

Child care. If you want to reach young families, you will have to develop an excellent preschool facility and program. If your arrangements are inadequate, those young families will not return. Consult available manuals that explain equipment, staffing, and policies. If you are uncertain about this, invite someone with advanced training in preschool education to visit your church and evaluate your current setup.

Conditions

I'm sure you have attended a worship service in a facility with distracting or uncomfortable physical conditions. For longtime members, these conditions may be a temporary annoyance, but for visitors they may be a real turnoff. Growing churches regulate worship conditions in order to enhance worship and impress guests.

Sound. Several years ago I visited a church with a new auditorium. The auditorium was truly beautiful, but I couldn't hear half of what was said. This was very frustrating to me and to others around me. I asked about the problem and was told that when the building funds ran short, the building committee chose a less expensive sound system. That compromise is easy to understand, but why build an auditorium if the worshipers can't hear the music or preaching?

Money invested in good equipment and expert advice is money well invested. If you are building a new facility, consult an audio engineer to be sure you provide the best sound.

Temperature. An auditorium that is too hot or too cold can hinder worship. Remember that a crowd of people gives off a lot of heat. An auditorium that feels comfortable before the service will feel too warm halfway through the sermon.

You may need to restrict access to the thermostat. I once preached in an auditorium where the thermostat was next to the pulpit platform. During the service four different people came to the front and adjusted the thermostat. Later, the custodian told me that the thermostat was broken. Hence, all of the adjustments made during the service were useless. If your auditorium is uncomfortable, you may need to consult a heating/cooling contractor for advice.

Seating. It seems that most church pews are designed to be uncomfortable. Many new churches are purchasing portable padded chairs or theater-type seating with individual padded seats. The advantage of the portable chairs is a flexible seating configuration. When people are comfortably seated, they will listen more attentively.

Lighting. Growing churches are concerned about the lighting in their buildings. I have preached in churches where the pulpit was so poorly lighted I could hardly read my Bible! Make sure that your pulpit area is brightly and attractively lighted. Also, check your exterior lighting. You will want to be sure that walkways and entrances are well lighted.

Cleanliness. Dirt and clutter make a poor impression on visitors. Take a periodic walk through your entire facility to be sure that everything looks clean and neat.

Evaluation. When he was pastor of the Green Valley Church in Birmingham, Alabama, Thom Rainer invited people who had never visited the church to walk through the facilities and share their impressions. When you see something all the time, you cease to notice it. A fresh look can be very revealing.

Accessibility

To our shame, most churches exclude handicapped persons because the facilities are not accessible to them. In order to make facilities accessible, we must give attention to walkways, curb cut-outs, ramps, elevators, doors, and parking. Manuals on making your building more accessible are available. You can evaluate your facility by inviting handicapped persons to tour it in order to identify problem areas. Almost 20 percent of the whole population is handicapped in some way. We can reach these people for Christ if we are sensitive to their physical needs.

MAKE A GOOD IMPRESSION

Before Rick Warren began holding services in Orange County, California, he visited over one thousand homes in the area. When he asked the people about the attitudes most people have toward churches, they listed these complaints:

1. Church is boring, and the sermons don't relate to my life.
2. Churches are unfriendly to visitors.
3. Churches are more interested in my money than in me.
4. Churches do not provide adequate child care.[8]

Visitors begin evaluating your church before the service begins. If they drive into your parking lot and find convenient spaces reserved for visitors, you've made a good start. If friendly greeters welcome and direct them, the first good impression is reinforced. If the building and grounds are clean and well kept, you've scored another point. If the people sitting near them welcome them with smiles and handshakes, then you have probably made a positive impression on your visitors.

Two years ago I visited Little Flock Church, one of the fastest-growing churches in the Louisville area. The church was conveniently located on a major highway. A large sign on the road helped me identify the church. The parking lot was well marked, and the visitors' parking area was easy to find. The design of the building funneled me toward the Welcome Center. A friendly greeter welcomed me and opened the door for me. To enter the auditorium I had to pass by the Welcome Center, where I received a worship program. When I sat down in the auditorium, several people smiled at me and welcomed me. When I spoke with the pastor, I commended him on the good impression the church made. It is no wonder that this church now holds two worship services and plans to double the size of its educational building.

The service should be user-friendly. Refer to your visitors as "guests." Don't embarrass them by making them stand up and tell their names. Allow them to be anonymous. Avoid "churchy" jargon that visitors will not understand. Simplify your worship program so that anyone can understand it. Lots of people don't know what an invocation and postlude are. Why not call them "opening prayer" and "organ music" instead. Reduce the time spent on announcements. Make only those announcements that are important to the entire congregation. If you do make announcements, explain them clearly. Veteran members know what VBS stands for, but many visitors don't. Many people believe churches are only interested in them for their money. Remember this when you take the offering; explain that the collection is merely a convenience for church members, and you do not expect guests to contribute. The key here is to think through the service from a guest's perspective.

DEVELOP A POSITIVE ATMOSPHERE

The atmosphere of worship can be defined as the "mood" or "spirit" of worship. However you define it, it is important. David Roozen and Kirk Hadaway say, "Churches that desire growth seem friendlier and more welcoming to newcomers. Such churches exude a different 'spirit' that visitors find attractive."[9] It is important to create a warm, appealing atmosphere in your worship services. Hadaway describes these services as joyful, expectant, celebrative, and revivalistic.[10]

Vance Havner said, "Most churches begin at eleven o'clock sharp and end at twelve o'clock dull." Outreach-oriented churches strive to avoid this at all costs. They try to create a feeling of enthusiasm and spontaneity during the service. Members of plateaued or declining churches describe their services as monotonous, boring, and formal.[11] Churches that desire to reach people for Christ must intentionally develop a worship atmosphere with several qualities:

Expectancy

When a service has expectancy, the people come in expecting something to happen. They expect to meet the living God, and they expect to see lives changed. There is an electric atmosphere like that in a basketball arena before a big game. The members enthusiastically come to worship because they are excited about what is going to happen. The pace of the service, attitude of the worship leaders, and temperament of the music all contribute to a lively atmosphere.

Intimacy

Growing churches develop a family atmosphere. The worshipers feel that they *belong* in this place with these people because they are accepted and affirmed.

Refreshment

Worship should recharge the worshipers' spiritual batteries and motivate them to serve the Lord during the following week. Instead of beating up your church members, encourage and restore them.

Spontaneity

Worshipers want to participate in a well-prepared service, but they also want the freedom to respond to the Spirit's leadership. Services that are overly rigid and formal do not attract visitors.

Warmth

The attitude the worship leaders project is vital. If they make the people feel warmly welcomed and cared for, then they have succeeded. Their tone of voice, facial expressions, and vocabulary all contribute to this.

PLAN YOUR WORSHIP

Target Your Audience

In order to plan for worship, you need to identify your target audience. Because people live longer now, some congregations are made up of people from four or even five generations. Obviously, these generations have different tastes in music and different "felt-needs." Churches like Willow Creek and Saddleback deliberately target baby boomers because this generation is the largest segment in the population (one-third). However, you may need to target another segment. If your church is located in a retirement community, you may need to target seniors. Or, if your church is located in a suburb with lots of young families, you may need to target baby busters. Many county-seat churches include a mixture of generations. In that case, you will need to determine which unchurched segment of the population you are trying to reach and plan worship services that will appeal to them.

Rick Warren suggests that you develop a profile of the typical person you are trying to reach. This profile includes age, lifestyle, interests, vocation, and education. Ask yourself, "How would Nashville Nick react to this worship service?" Then find out which radio stations your target group listens to. If you are trying to reach young urban adults, you probably ought to feature contemporary Christian music. Identifying a target group will also help you choose sermon topics and appropriate illustrations.

Worship Styles

People need a church in which they feel comfortable. Rick Warren writes, "The style of worship that you feel comfortable with says far more about your cultural background than it does about your theology. Debates over worship style are almost always sociological and personality debates couched in theological terms."[12] The better you understand your target group, the better you will be able to plan worship that speaks to them. Here are the types of worship typically found in North America:

Liturgical. This style usually follows the prescribed seasons of the church year, such as Advent, Lent, etc. It is frequently found in Episcopal and Lutheran congregations and emphasizes formality and order. The music is typically classical, performed by a trained choir and played on a pipe organ. The order of worship seldom changes, and it includes readings (lessons) from the Old and New Testaments, printed or read prayers, responsive readings, choral responses, and periods of quiet meditation.

Traditional. This style is commonly found in older evangelical churches. The order of worship varies little from week to week. It includes an organ or piano prelude, invocation, welcome, hymns (sung from the hymnal), announcements, offering, choir special, Scripture reading, sermon, invitation, benediction, and postlude.

Blended. This style is growing in popularity. It seeks to blend elements from contemporary worship with the traditional style. The hope is that unchurched worship guests will enjoy the service, while longtime church members will not feel alienated. Blended worship incorporates some praise choruses in the service along with contemporary solos, occasional drama, and practical sermons.

Contemporary. Contemporary worship seeks to appeal to younger people. Worshipers and leaders often dress casually. The services feature contemporary music, especially praise choruses, that are often projected on large screens. Hymnals are used little, if at all. Accompaniment is provided by electric pianos, synthesizers, electric guitars, and drums. Many contemporary services include a drama. This drama introduces an issue in modern life that the pastor addresses in the sermon. Sermons are brief; they incorporate lots of humor and avoid theological jargon and heavy exegesis. In many churches there is no pulpit, and some churches have a stage rather than a platform.

The following chart was developed by Glen Martin. It illustrates the differences between traditional worship and contemporary worship.

Traditional	Contemporary
Hymns	Praise songs
Organ/piano	Small band
Hymn books	Overheads/slides
Song leader	Worship leader
Slower pacing	Faster pacing
Quietness	Talking
Softer sounds	Louder sounds
Longer service	Shorter service
Sermon	Message
Standard format	Variable format
Bulletin	Worship folder
Soft lighting	Bright lighting
Contemplation	Celebration
Choir	Praise team
Content-oriented	Heart-oriented
Sanctuary	Auditorium
Audio orientation	Visual orientation
Varied talent used	Best talent used
Haphazard service	Rehearsed service
Little Planning	Much planning[13]

African-American. Worship in African-American churches is joyful and celebrative. Worshipers interact with the preacher and music. The services are typically spontaneous and often last two hours or more. The worshipers' warm enthusiasm is complemented by powerful preaching.

Characteristics of a Good Worship Service

Good worship demonstrates several characteristics:

A good worship service is joyful. The service ought to lead the worshipers to rejoice in the Lord's presence and blessings (Pss. 122:1; 100:2,4).

A good worship service exalts Christ. Everything done in the service should glorify him.

A good worship service is thematic. The key elements of the service should relate to a theme, which is determined by the sermon topic. I once attended a service in which the theme for the hymns was the cross; the theme for the special music was the second coming; and the sermon theme was stewardship. The service would have been better had it been planned around the stewardship theme.

A good worship service is orderly. Good worship should be planned, prepared, and practiced (see 1 Cor. 14:40). Our God deserves our best efforts. Most worshipers spend only one hour a week at church. We must use the time fully and wisely. Notice how much information is conveyed in a thirty-minute newscast. This was possible because the newscast was carefully planned and prepared. A worship service can be both well-planned and spontaneous. This is accomplished by following the plan, but also by being open and sensitive to the leading of the Holy Spirit.

A good worship service is stimulating. It speaks both to the heart and mind and avoids boring repetition through the use of variety in its order. Some churches have used the same order of service so long that the worshipers can function on automatic pilot.

A good worship service is participative. Worship should involve the entire congregation. To truly worship, one must participate. Leaders should give much time to thinking about how to involve the congregation more fully.

A good worship service is well paced. Most services drag. Leaders should seek to eliminate dead time, periods when nothing is happening. I once preached in a church where an elderly deacon led the prayer. When it was time for him to pray, he walked very slowly from his seat in the tenth row to the pulpit. This took several minutes. In another church the deacon who led in prayer sat on the platform and stepped up beside the minister of music as the hymn concluded. As soon as the hymn ended, the deacon prayed. There was no dead time at all. Good planning makes for smooth transitions throughout the service.

A good worship service challenges worshipers to commitment. Worship should do more than inform or entertain; it should effect changes in people's lives.

Elements of Worship

Worship services take on varied forms, but all have certain common elements.

Music. Music is the most controversial aspect of worship. The style and mood of the music you choose is greatly determined by the worship service. Evangelistic churches choose music that is warmhearted, that is, it speaks to the heart. The music should also be lively.

Preaching. Growing churches feature strong biblical preaching. Evangelistic pastors emphasize the authority of the Scriptures, and they apply God's Word to the needs of their congregations. They know their needs because they spend time with their people. Rick Warren suggests that pastors preach short series of sermons with appealing titles. Advertising the series may attract the unchurched. It is also helpful to provide an outline with the Scriptures for the sermon printed out.[14]

According to James Emery White, preaching that reaches people is:

- *Targeted.* The messages are targeted at the people the church is trying to reach.

- *Biblical.* The sermons highlight biblical text; they are largely expository.

- *Practical.* The sermons speak to life issues and emphasize application.

- *Relevant.* The messages touch the people according to where they are in their lives.

- *Interesting.* The sermons feature creative illustrations and humor.

- *Simple.* The preacher uses a simple outline, speaks in a conversational style, and avoids religious jargon.

- *Positive.* The preacher emphasizes what the church stands for, not what it is against.[15]

Scripture reading. The unchurched do not understand the King James Version. Therefore, it is important to use a modern translation. Also, make a pew (or chair) Bible available, because many visitors will not bring a Bible with them. It may be helpful to tell them the page number as many will not know biblical notation. Finally, select texts that are not difficult to understand.

Prayer. The prayer leader should lead or guide the people to pray themselves, not just listen. The prayers should be conversational and simple. Long prayers with flowery language have no place in an evangelistic church.

Testimony. In the past, evangelical churches used the testimony more than they do now. Today, many growing churches ask new Christians to give testimonies about how they were saved. The testimony is a powerful tool for telling others about God's grace. Testimonies need to be brief and to the point.

Giving. We need to emphasize that giving is a part of worship. By giving we express our love and devotion to God.

Ordinances. We do not usually think of the ordinances as evangelistic events, but they can be. Baptism is a public testimony of the new believer's faith in Christ. Yet, we normally conduct baptisms inside the church where few (if any) lost people see.

When I served as a missionary in the Philippines, we normally held baptisms at a public beach in the context of an evangelistic service. During the service, we would sing gospel songs and listen to the testimonies of the new believers. In addition, an evangelistic message would be preached. Lots of people would crowd around to see what we were doing. Instruct the candidates for baptism to invite their lost friends and relatives, and make the baptismal service evangelistic.

Invitation. It is important to give worshipers an opportunity to respond to the message. This may be done by inviting them to "walk the aisle" and come to the front of the church for counseling or by registering their decision on a card in the pew (or both). Either way, it is important to counsel with those making decisions for Christ.

John Bisagno, pastor of the First Baptist Church of Houston, makes these suggestions about giving the invitation:

- *Give the invitation prayerfully.* The preacher must be sensitive to the leadership of the Holy Spirit, and this sensitivity begins with prayer before the service. The preacher should also pray for those who need to make decisions.

- *Give the invitation authoritatively.* Don't be hesitant or timid; speak with conviction as God's spokesperson.

- *Explain clearly.* Many people hesitate to respond because they are uncertain about what will happen. Explain what an invitation is and what will happen to those who respond.

- *Give different invitations.* A good invitation has more than one part. You may want to invite people to be saved, to join the church, to dedicate their lives to Christian service, to repent, or to express a special need.

- *Give the invitation urgently.* Emphasize the call of God to accept Christ today.

- *Give the invitation smoothly.* Discuss the invitation with the musicians before the service. Agree on the invitation song and signals that you will use.

- *Give the people time to respond.* Bisagno states that 90 percent of converts come forward after the third verse of the invitation hymn. Too many preachers end the invitation after two verses.

- *Give the invitation positively.* Avoid any type of negative statement. Don't say, "If you are going to come"; instead, say, "When you come" or "As you come." Bo Baker, an experienced evangelist, says, "You know you are going to come; as you do, we will wait for you."

- *Plan the invitation.* Think about how you will move from your sermon's conclusion into the invitation.

- *Deal carefully with those who come forward.* I have counseled with many people who responded to the invitation just to get attention, be patted on the back, and asked to fill out a card. Walking the aisle does not make a person a Christian; it just shows that he or she is under conviction. Be sure that someone reads the Scriptures and prays with everyone who responds.[16]

Planning Procedure

Worship planning is essential. Some churches plan far in advance, while others do not plan at all. The best procedure to follow is to do general planning six months in advance and specific planning a week before the worship service. In most churches the church staff plans the services, but some churches have a worship committee. Music preparation is much easier when the pastor develops a plan for preaching and informs the appropriate parties of his plan.

The bulletin, worship folder, or program is an important part of the worship experience. It should guide the worshipers, especially guests, through the worship service. Visitors typically do not know what to expect; this makes them nervous. A well-designed worship folder will allay these apprehensions. Lay out the design with visitors in mind. Bulletins are now available with detachable attendance forms. Many churches ask everyone who attends to fill out these forms–members and guests alike. This practice will help you identify prospects for visitation and keep track of the attendance of your members. Your average worship attendance is an important measure of church health.

The folder should tell something about your church, present the plan of salvation, and explain how to join the church.

Scheduling Services

The services should be scheduled at times that are most convenient for the greatest number of people. Most evangelicals think eleven o'clock on Sunday morning is a holy time. However, churches set that time years ago in order to accommodate the farmers who had to do their morning chores before they hitched up their wagon and drove to church. Now only two percent of Americans work as farmers, but we have kept the old schedule. How can you know what time people prefer? Ask them. You can survey your congregation and community to find out what time or times would best accommodate their schedules.

Most churches could reach more people by offering multiple services. Catholic churches have done this for years by offering masses at several different times each week. William Easum says churches will grow "with the addition of each new morning worship service."[17] In 1980 the Alamo United Methodist Church in San Antonio, Texas, began a second service, and attendance increased from 68 to 93 in six months. Later a third service was added, and total attendance increased to 168 within six months. The principle is this: The more convenient your worship schedule is, the more people will come.

157

CONSIDER A SEEKER SERVICE

Many churches are developing *seeker services* to reach the lost. A seeker service is a service designed to attract secular people to the church. Willow Creek Community Church in Chicago originated the seeker service. Bill Hybels, the pastor, found it difficult to evangelize the lost and edify the saints in the same service. So, he divided the services. Willow Creek offers worship services for believers on Wednesday and Thursday nights, but the Saturday night and Sunday morning services target "seekers" (unchurched adults).

When Hybels and his staff studied Chicago's unchurched population, they discovered that these people desired the following qualities in a church:

1. Anonymity—they wanted to visit church without being "recognized" or singled out.

2. Clarity and Simplicity—they wanted the sermon and service to be easily understood.

3. Relevance—they wanted to hear sermons about practical life issues.

4. Excellence—they expected quality performance.

5. Freedom—they wanted time to make up their minds without pressure.[18]

In order to reach these people, Willow Creek developed a new type of service that includes contemporary music, drama, multimedia presentation, and a topical message that addresses a concern of the unchurched. The staff presupposes that the people attending know nothing about Christ or Christianity.

Should your church implement a seeker service? Realistically, most churches do not have the resources to develop one. A quality service requires creative people who can present dramas and skilled musicians who can perform contemporary music. Seeker services require more planning and practice than traditional services. Ed Dobson, author of *Starting a Seeker-Sensitive Service,* writes:

> Don't start a seeker-sensitive service to get more people inside the church. Don't start a seeker-sensitive service because you feel a need to change. Don't start a seeker-sensitive service because Willow Creek does it. Don't start a seeker-sensitive service because it is the "in" thing to do. Don't start a seeker-sensitive service because people in the

church want you to do it. Don't start a seeker-sensitive service because you would like to do it. Start a seeker-sensitive service because you have a personal and all-consuming passion for people who don't know the Lord.[19]

If your church has the personnel and the passion, then you may want to develop a seeker service. Whether you do or not, studying seeker-service principles can help you make traditional or blended services more user-friendly.

Some writers distinguish between a seeker service and a seeker-sensitive service. A *seeker-sensitive service* is more traditional, but the planners keep the needs and concerns of seekers in mind while also attempting to satisfy longtime church members. Those who plan a true *seeker service* do not concern themselves with the comfort zone of longtime members. Instead, they do everything with the unchurched in mind.

EVALUATE YOUR WORSHIP

Most manufacturing companies have quality control departments by which they endeavor to ensure the quality of their products by constant testing. Churches do well to evaluate their services periodically. There are three ways to do this:

1. Make a videotape of your service. View the tape and analyze each aspect of the service. Notice especially the pace of the service and the vocabulary used. Ask: What could we do to improve?

2. Arrange for someone to visit your service and evaluate it. You could ask someone from the local association, a state convention staff member, a professor, or a retired minister. It would be good to provide an evaluation sheet so the person knows what to look for. Another way to do this is to send a videotape to a worship expert for evaluation.

3. Distribute evaluation forms to visitors and members. The comments from visitors can help you know how user-friendly the service is. Comments of regular attenders will tell you how satisfied they are with the services. If your church has a worship committee, the committee members can take the lead in the survey and help you interpret the responses.

CHANGE YOUR WORSHIP

You have already learned that most churches need to change in order to grow and reach people for Christ. Many need to change their worship in order to reach the lost. This is much easier said than done, especially when we consider the fact that the first murder in the Bible was over the correct style of worship. It is easier to plant a new church than to change an old one. Typically, music is the most controversial element of worship. Keep your target group in your own mind, and in the minds of your members.

As you change your worship, keep these pointers in mind:

Move slowly in changing worship. It is better to take baby steps at first. Monitor the church members' responses to change. If you seem to be moving too fast, slow down a bit.

Affirm those who disagree. By your actions and attitude, show the dissenting members that you love them and respect their opinions and feelings.

Offer services with different styles. For example, you may decide to offer a contemporary service at 8:30 A.M. and a traditional service at 11:00 A.M.

Organize a worship committee. The committee can advise you and help to absorb some of the negative reaction.[20]

SUMMARY

Worship has replaced Sunday school as the "front door" to the church. You can make your services more appealing to the lost and unchurched by making them user-friendly and by maintaining attractive facilities. Take care to make a good first impression. Growing churches develop a friendly, expectant, and revivalistic atmosphere.

Choose a style of worship that will appeal to your target group. Plan and practice your worship so it will be orderly and excellent. Every worship service should be built around the theme of the sermon. The sermon is the key element of the service. It should be biblically based and practically focused. To reach more people in worship, offer more services in different styles. Seeker services are a popular and effective means to reach the lost through worship. Evaluate your worship to see if you are accomplishing your goals. If you decide to change your church's worship, proceed with caution and enlist the help of a worship committee to implement changes.

STUDY QUESTIONS

1. What is the definition of worship?
2. What must the church do to make a good first impression on visitors?
3. What are the five styles of worship?
4. What are the keys to worship planning?
5. How can worship services be evaluated?

FOR FURTHER STUDY

Dobson, Ed. *Starting a Seeker-Sensitive Service.* Grand Rapids: Zondervan Publishing House, 1993.

Easum, William M. *The Church Growth Handbook.* Nashville: Abingdon Press, 1990.

Hayford, Jack, John Killinger, and Howard Stevenson. *Mastering Worship.* Portland: Multnomah Press, 1990.

Morgenthaler, Sally. *Worship Evangelism.* Grand Rapids: Zondervan Publishing House, 1995.

White, James Emery. *Opening the Front Door: Worship and Church Growth.* Nashville: Convention Press, 1992.

CHAPTER 12

REACH THE COMMUNITY
THROUGH THE MEDIA

≫ ———————— ≪

In this chapter we will study ways to use mass media to reach the lost and unchurched. The first part of the chapter will deal with church advertising and the second part will be devoted to media evangelism. Certainly, mass media represents a valuable resource for churches and Christian organizations. Understanding this fact is easy. The hard part is deciding which type of media to use and how to use it. When you finish the chapter, I hope you will be able to answer these questions for your church. Lots of churches waste money on media because they have not done the research and planning necessary to make their use of mass media effective. Good stewardship of resources requires that we spend the Lord's money wisely and to the greatest effect.

THE BASIC PRINCIPLE OF CHURCH ADVERTISING

Here is the basic principle of church advertising: *People can only come to your church if they know it exists.* I once visited a woman who lived two blocks from my church in Dallas, Texas. This was a large church that had been at the same location for sixty years. When I told her I was from Calvary Baptist Church, she asked, "Where is your church?" Obviously, we had done a poor job of publicizing our church's location. People need to know your church's name and location if they are going to attend it.

STEPS TO EFFECTIVE CHURCH ADVERTISING

Churches can use their advertising dollars most effectively by following these five steps:

Step #1: Determine Your Image

Successful advertising features a memorable slogan. You will need to develop a slogan that projects the image of your church you want the community to receive. If you are trying to reach unchurched people, you will want to avoid "churchy" jargon and you will want to consider what will attract them to your church. If your church features contemporary worship, you will want to emphasize that. Work with creative people in your congregation to develop a slogan and a logo. If your church members lack this expertise, consult a professional advertising or marketing firm. It is money well spent.

Step #2: Choose Your Target Audience

You should aim your advertising at a particular group of people. Do you want to reach young couples with children or senior citizens? Once you answer this question, you will know how to prepare your advertisements and where to place them. Most large cities have a radio station that plays music from the 1930s, 40s, and 50s. This station appeals mainly to older folks. Guess which businesses advertise with this station? Chiropractors, eye clinics, travel agencies, and funeral homes. Who advertises on the rock stations? Music stores and night clubs. In order to target effectively, develop a description of the typical person you are trying to reach with your advertising. Your slogan and logo should appeal to that person. How can you know whether they do or not? After you've come up with a slogan and logo (or more than one of each), ask selected people who are like those in your target group if the slogan and logo are appealing or not.

Step #3: Choose Your Media Mix

A combination of advertising media is usually more effective than only one. Using radio, television, newspapers, and billboards in a coordinated campaign is the most effective.[1]

Step #4: Emphasize Quality

Many churches try to save money by doing the ads or radio spots themselves. The results often defeat their purpose. Churches do better to emphasize quality rather than quantity. A professionally prepared piece will be more attractive and cost effective.

Step #5: Evaluate Results

It is hard to know how well your advertising is working. One way to discover this is to ask guests in your worship service how they learned about your church. Your visitor's card might read like this:

How did you learn about our church? Please check one:
- ❏ Radio
- ❏ Television
- ❏ Newspaper
- ❏ Billboard
- ❏ Family Member
- ❏ Friend.

Make your own list according to the forms of media you are using. The answers you receive will show you which media are most effective for your church. You will want to include family and friends in the list because word-of-mouth advertising is important. In fact, it is the best kind.[2]

Evaluating your advertising will help you to select appropriate forms of media and to budget for advertising. I've noticed that when I purchase a new appliance, the warranty card always includes a survey asking how I learned about the product. Obviously, General Electric employs this principle of evaluation.

I hope your church has not committed any of these sins. What should your church be doing? The following are some positive ways to publicize your church.

WAYS TO ADVERTISE YOUR CHURCH

There are many ways to advertise your church. The list below illustrates some of them, but it is not exhaustive. Your church's location, size, and budget will determine which methods you choose. The important thing is that you use some of these methods.

Advertise in Your Local Paper

Almost every city and town in the United States has a local paper. Some of these are daily and others are weekly. Nevertheless,

Figure 12.1

CHEYNEY'S SEVEN SINS OF ADVERTISING

Many churches commit one or more of the *Seven Sins of Advertising* listed by Tom Cheyney:

1. *Bragging.* A lost person doesn't care that your church led the state convention in baptisms.

2. *Talking to yourself.* Church advertising should address the unchurched, not church members.

3. *Preaching.* Preaching is appropriate in the pulpit, but it is not effective in advertising.

4. *Being Noisy.* Noise just gives people a headache. Your advertising should accomplish a purpose.

5. *Being Sloppy.* Often advertising is done at the last minute, and the haste shows. Cheyney says, "Go for class, not mass."

6. *Trying to Be Cute.* Humor is often ineffective because some people don't understand it. Ask people in your target group to preview your advertising and give you an honest evaluation.

7. *Being Dull or Boring.* Good advertising has a "hook" that catches the public's interest.[3]

they all offer you a way to communicate with your community. The cost of an ad will vary according to the newspaper's circulation and the size of an ad. Newspapers sell ads by the column inch. The more column inches your ad takes up, the higher the cost.

Keep several things in mind when designing and purchasing newspaper advertising. First, repeat the ad at least once a week, preferably on Saturday, for four consecutive weeks. Repetition will reinforce your message. However, after about a month you will need to change the ad because people will stop noticing it. Second, try to avoid the "church page." Ask the editor if the ad can be placed in the family news or general news section. Also, ask for a position on the outside border rather than on the inner crease.

Third, select a newspaper that reaches the most homes in your community at the lowest cost to you. Many suburban communities have a weekly paper. That paper may be more effective for your church than the metropolitan daily. Fourth, remember that newspapers are businesses that must make a profit to survive. If you pay for advertising regularly, then the editor will be more open to printing news stories or photos that you submit.

Here are some pointers for preparing appealing ads. First, the ad should attract the attention of your target group. Second, it should turn the reader's attention into interest. Third, it should move the reader from merely interest to a stimulating desire to participate. Fourth, the ad should encourage the reader to make a specific response: attend church, come to the concert, or whatever. Fifth, it should be written in language the unchurched can understand.[4]

BUY SPOTS ON LOCAL RADIO

Radio commercials are called "spots." A church can buy fifteen-thirty-, or sixty-second spots. Thirty-second spots are the best buy. All radio stations keep records about their ratings (the size of their listening audience). Stations with a larger listening audience charge more for spots. The timing of the spot also affects the price. If you place your spot during "drive time" (when people are commuting to work), you will pay more. Spots that are before, during, or after newscasts are also more costly.

You should choose the radio station according to the audience you hope to reach. If your town has only one station, the choice is easy. However, if you live in an urban area, you may have twenty stations to choose from. If you want to reach blue-collar workers, you may want to choose a country-western station. If you want to reach baby boomers (like me), you may need to choose a rock-and-roll "oldies" station. Many pastors feel they need to support the local Christian station so they put spots on that station. However, the unchurched seldom listen to a Christian station. To reach them, you'll have to find out what stations they prefer. How can you learn this? Ask them.

Use professionals to prepare your spots. Local stations employ professionals to prepare spots all the time, and they will gladly prepare spots for you. Usually, the cost of production is included in the cost of airtime. Be sure to preview the spot before it airs. If it does not communicate your message, insist that it be revised. Don't try to include too much in the spot. Focus on one service or event. Be sure your church's name and address are clearly identified.[5]

Purchase Local Television Spots

Television advertising is much more expensive than radio spots, and television production costs are not included in the spot rates. Your denomination may be able to help you with this. Again, professionalism is essential; a spot you make yourself may turn people off rather than attract them. Realistically, most churches cannot afford to use television. If your church can, run your spot in connection with a program popular with your target group. If you want to reach children, advertise on a Saturday morning cartoon show. If you want to reach young men, advertise on a sporting event. Week by week the local newscasts attract the largest audience. Of course, the stations charge more for those time slots.[6]

Use Billboards

The use of billboards is a popular way to communicate with drivers. However, before you agree to a contract with an advertising company, ask about the billboard's location and how many cars pass by each day. Also, you'll want to know if the sign is lighted at night. Your ad should be simple and feature your church's logo. You can't use many words on a billboard because people are only driving by; thus, they will only have a short time to read your message.[7]

Distribute Promotional Items

If your church develops a logo, you can print that logo on bumper stickers, yard signs, pencils, pens, key chains, and balloons. I mentioned the Southeast Christian Church in an earlier chapter. This church prints bumper stickers that can be found throughout the Louisville area. They read, "Follow Me to Southeast Church." At Christmas the Shively Baptist Church printed yard signs that promoted the church's annual pageant.

Participate in Community Events

Another way to promote your church is through participation in community events. One church sponsored a booth at the county fair that provided cold water and a place to sit and rest. Those who stopped by also received a gospel tract and a brochure about the church. Members who staffed the booth also gave away promotional items bearing the church's name and address.

Other churches participate in parades. I know one church that always builds a float for the town's Christmas parade. The theme of the float centers on the true meaning of Christmas. Participating in an activity like a parade shows that your church is active and involved in the community.

Your church can attract favorable attention by hosting community events. You should also consider presenting awards to public servants and seeking media coverage for the event. One church presents an annual award to the firefighter of the year. The firefighter is given the award at a ceremony, and all the firefighters are honored for their sacrificial service. This annual event has prompted a very positive response in the community.

Take Advantage of Free Publicity

Most churches don't have much money for advertising. However, there are many free ways to advertise your church. Most radio stations offer a community calendar program. During this program, a list of upcoming community events is read. There is no cost for this service. Ask your local station how to go about getting your church's activities listed in this public service information.

Local papers are always happy to print local news. If you prepare brief, well-written news stories about your church's activities, the paper will often use them. Also, buy a camera, keep black-and-white film in it. Take photos and send an occasional photo to the local paper, along with a caption identifying the people pictured. Finally, some papers will include a regular column written by a local pastor. If you are interested, ask the editor about this.

Reach People through Direct Mail

We all receive direct mail advertising. Businesses use direct mail to sell all types of things. Direct mail can help you locate prospects who are interested in what your church can offer. Direct mail can help your church:

- Target a specific group of people.
- Reach the target group with a message of special interest.
- Communicate your church's image.
- Prompt immediate response by prospects.

- Change negative perceptions into positive ones.
- Measure the campaign's effectiveness.[8]

Direct mail can be expensive, and most small churches cannot afford it. However, it can help urban and suburban churches deliver a message to their communities. If you decide that direct mail could help your church, you will want to follow these steps in order to reach your community while practicing good stewardship in the process.

Step #1: Clarify your purpose and set a clear objective. You must identify your target group by asking two questions: (1) Who do we wish to reach? (2) What do we want our prospects to do? If you want them to come to a concert, you will take one approach; but, if you want young adults to come to a parenting seminar, you will take another approach.

Step #2: Develop a mailing list (or lists). You can find the names of companies that sell mailing lists under the heading "Mailing Lists" in the yellow pages. The lists these companies provide identify all different types of people: home owners, singles, students, retirees, renters, and newcomers. You can also acquire a list of all the households in a given geographic area. Mailing list companies can even provide you with adhesive mailing labels by postal carrier route.

Do you want to use a rifle approach or do you prefer a shotgun approach? If you are advertising a new worship service, then a shotgun mailing to all the residents in a given area would be appropriate. If you are trying to attract young parents to a new preschool, you will spend your money more wisely by using a rifle mailing to households with children. The postage rates for a shotgun mailing are cheaper.

Step #3: Compose an attractive mailing. Many churches try to load too much information on a single mailing. It is better to keep each mailing simple and use it to communicate just one event or program. The piece should be designed and laid out by a professional, if possible. You may have someone in your church who can offer these services. It is better to use colored paper for mailings. Some churches have found that people are more likely to read cards than letters in envelopes.

Step #4: Ascertain your effectiveness. If you advertise for a special event, ask visitors how they learned of the event. You can do this orally or with a guest response card.

Step #5: Keep on communicating. You may have to mail several pieces to reach some people. By designing a series of mailings, you may shape the community's perception of your church. Remember that people act of the basis of what they perceive to be true. Your church may be very friendly, but if the unchurched people in your town think otherwise, they won't come.[9]

What kind of results can you expect? The advertising company may be able to advise you of the response rate in your area; of course it will vary from place to place and according to the quality of the brochure. I spoke with a pastor from the Detroit area whose church mails out ten thousand brochures to the people in his suburban community two or three times a year. The brochures are designed by a professional who donates his time. The pastor said that fifty new worshipers come to the church after each mailing. Not all the fifty become members, but he feels the expense is worth the money and effort.

Mass media can help you fulfill the important function of informing your community about your church and its ministries, but you can also use the media to communicate the gospel of Christ. That is the focus of the following section.

PRINCIPLES OF MEDIA EVANGELISM

Mass media is a means by which you can reach masses of people. Jesus and Paul even used mass media by going to places where there were large numbers of people. Jesus traveled from town to town and from village to village. Paul preached in the marketplaces, synagogues, and even on Mars Hill. Adrian Rogers, pastor of Bellevue Baptist Church near Memphis, says, "We need to be taking the church into the marketplace."[10] Mass media can take you where the people are.

Many churches try to communicate the gospel by means of the mass media, but very few communicate effectively. Media evangelism is expensive, and lots of money is wasted. If your church decides to develop a media ministry, keep the following principles in mind:

Principle #1

Almost all Americans watch television and listen to the radio every day. Obviously, radio and television can deliver a message to the masses very quickly. That is why companies spend millions to advertise their products on radio and television. If you want to reach a large number of people with a brief message, radio and television are the way to do it. Without doubt, mass media can enhance evangelism.

Principle #2

Mass media cannot replace personal involvement. When churches first began televising worship services, many thought that people would soon stop coming to the church building to worship. Some sports-writers expressed the same opinion when baseball games were first televised. Of course, neither prediction proved true. People want to be involved personally. A television or radio program can't shake your hand or give you a hug. Media can only be effective in evangelism when there is some kind of personal follow-up with those who are making decisions. The following figures are revealing.[11]

Figure 12.2

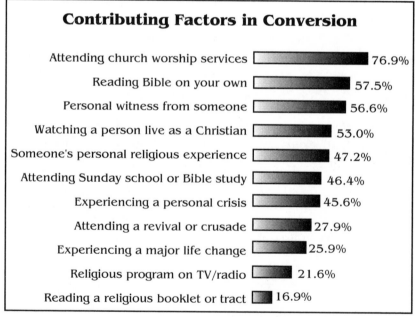

Contributing Factors in Conversion

Attending church worship services	76.9%
Reading Bible on your own	57.5%
Personal witness from someone	56.6%
Watching a person live as a Christian	53.0%
Someone's personal religious experience	47.2%
Attending Sunday school or Bible study	46.4%
Experiencing a personal crisis	45.6%
Attending a revival or crusade	27.9%
Experiencing a major life change	25.9%
Religious program on TV/radio	21.6%
Reading a religious booklet or tract	16.9%

Principle #3

Target your programs to lost people. Many church programs I see and hear do not appeal to the lost. They miss their intended audience for two basic reasons. First, they broadcast on the wrong stations. Lots of programs intended to reach the lost are aired on

Christian stations. These stations certainly deserve our support. They minister to Christians, but few lost people listen to or watch these stations. If you want to reach the lost, you need to know what stations they like. The top radio station in the Dallas/Fort Worth market is a country-western station. Research conducted by Jeffrey Hadden revealed that the people who view "televangelists" are mostly older, female (60–73%), and already church members.[12]

Second, the content, format, and vocabulary used in their programs are not designed to attract the lost. Thus, the programs are simply not attractive to them. If you are unsure about what to do, seek professional advice and ask some lost or unchurched people for their opinion of a pilot program.

Principle #4

Invite your viewers/hearers to call or write to someone. It is important to personalize the program as much as possible. When you conclude the program, encourage the people to write to the speaker or "star" of the program. This will help both the listeners and you. It will enable you to provide the listeners with counseling and literature, and it will give you a reading on prospects your program is reaching.

Principle #5

Establish a logo and a slogan. If you want your program to help build your church, you need to develop a logo and a slogan. Use the logo and slogan on your programs, billboards, stationery, church bulletins, bumper stickers, yard signs, and your church sign. Repetition is a key to communication.

Principle #6

Quality is more important than quantity. You would do better to develop one special program, produced with excellence, than to broadcast an amateurish weekly program. The cable company that serves our city provides one channel for free public access. Many of the programs on this channel are presented by churches, but the quality is embarrassing. I can't imagine a lost person watching them, much less being attracted to Christ. If you are going to do it, do it right.

Principle #7

If you want to reach a city, you must get on TV regularly. Television helps you develop both name and face recognition. If you are widely recognized you can become the city's pastor.[13]

Principle #8

Personal testimonies are effective in reaching lost persons. Few techniques are more effective than the personal testimony which can be used in many settings, including radio and television. Be sure that the people you choose practice and time their testimonies before going on the air.

Principle #9

Complex messages are hard to communicate by radio and television. Newscasters are always looking for a "sound bite," a short, pithy statement that conveys a message. If you want to communicate the gospel by radio and television, you must master this technique.

Principle #10

Visual images are important. The younger generations are visually oriented. A "talking head" television program may have little more effect than a radio program. Use visual images to communicate the message of salvation.

Principle #11

The message of salvation is always more important than the medium. Too many churches and ministries have compromised the gospel by allowing the demands of the medium to affect the purity of their doctrine. We must present the gospel in an attractive way, but never compromise the truth.

APPROACHES TO MEDIA EVANGELISM

Churches take many different approaches to media evangelism. Probably the most effective approach is to use a mixture of media. Broadmoor Baptist Church in Shreveport, Louisiana, is a church noted for its media ministry. Pastor Mark Brister says, "At Broadmoor we use a media mix and many different approaches in our efforts to touch people with the gospel. Because of our use of media, people know us."[14] Broadmoor broadcasts its morning and evening services on the ACTS cable channel. Thirty minutes of the morning service is also broadcast on the local ABC affiliate and a local radio station. In addition, the church places spots on radio and television. Furthermore, the church's billboards have attracted national attention. Next to a billboard for Harrah's Casino the church erected its own billboard, featuring a picture of the Bible with the caption, "The only sure bet in town!"

Radio

Radio is much less expensive than television both to produce and to broadcast. The only way to get on popular stations during prime time is to buy spots. Ask broadcasting professionals to help you produce these spots. Many small-town churches broadcast their services on the radio. This can be a service to shut-ins, but I wonder if it has much impact on the lost. If you want to reach the lost, try another format—like a call-in show or interview program.

Television

Television can take you into the homes of your community. It is an expensive way to get there, though. Many large churches broadcast their Sunday services. Like the radio, this is a blessing to home-bound folks. It can also be a way for people to try out your church and to develop recognition in the community. Mark Brister went to visit a church member in the hospital, but he was given the wrong room number. When he opened the door, a man he didn't know sat up, looking surprised, and a woman sitting near the bed stood up and said, "Oh, Dr. Mark, we just knew you would come." This couple had watched Broadmoor's broadcasts, and they had prayed that Dr. Brister would visit them in the hospital.[15] If you do broadcast your service, emphasize the church's name and location at the beginning and end of each broadcast. Also, invite the viewers to write the pastor to share their concerns.

In addition to broadcasting their Sunday services, many churches produce spots that air at various times. Some churches also produce Easter and Christmas specials.

Cable Television

Cable television offers smaller churches an opportunity to reach their communities. It is easier and cheaper to place a program on a local cable channel than on a major network. In fact, some small-town systems allow churches to broadcast at no cost. Laypersons can perform the technical tasks required to accomplish this, but you would do well to bring in professional technicians to train them.

SUMMARY

Church media ministry includes both advertising and evangelism. Both are important. You need to inform your community about your church because people can't come if they don't know it exists. Use your advertising budget wisely; determine your target audience and use the form or forms of media that will most effectively reach it. Don't be timid about asking for advice. If you don't have trained people in your church, consult with professionals.

Christians spend a lot of money on "gospel broadcasting," but few lost people listen to it. Find out what the lost do listen to and use those stations to communicate the gospel to them. A mixture of media is best both for advertising and evangelism. Whatever approach you choose, take it to where the people are.

STUDY QUESTIONS

1. What is the basic principle of church advertising?
2. Why is it important to identify a target audience?
3. Why is a mixture of different forms of media advantageous?
4. How can spots be more effective than programs?
5. Why is the personal testimony such a powerful tool?

FOR FURTHER STUDY

Barna, George. *Marketing the Church.* Colorado Springs: NavPress, 1988.

Benson, Dennis. *The Visible Church.* Nashville: Abingdon Press, 1988.

Engel, James F. *How Can I Get Them to Listen?* Grand Rapids: Zondervan Publishing House, 1977.

Kiser, Wayne. *Promotion Strategies for the Local Church.* Nashville: Broadman Press, 1992.

CHAPTER 13

SCHEDULE SPECIAL EVENTS

Effective evangelistic churches emphasize evangelism in their planning, promotion, preaching, and programming. George Barna surveyed a number of growing, evangelistic churches and discovered twelve elements common to all:

1. They have an evangelistic culture driven by the pastor.
2. Their philosophy of ministry has evangelism at its core.
3. Their mission and vision emphasize evangelism.
4. Their weekend services are highly evangelistic.
5. They use evangelistic events frequently and strategically.
6. They steal their best ideas from other churches.
7. They spend money on outreach.
8. They are innovative, risk-taking, aggressive, and restless.
9. They provide good evangelistic training.
10. Their congregations are networked with non-Christians.
11. They set significant evangelistic goals.
12. They cooperate with other churches for God's purposes.[1]

We have already discussed many of these elements. In this chapter we will focus on special evangelistic events.

Why are special events important to a church's evangelism strategy? Special events help you reach those who have not been drawn by the church's regular programs. In another survey David Schmidt learned that large events are "the primary way people enter churches." Special events like crusades, concerts, dramas, and sports activities attract the unchurched. Churches that want to reach people for Christ must develop creative ways of catching the attention of non-Christians.[2]

ADVANTAGES AND DISADVANTAGES

Every approach to evangelism has advantages and disadvantages. Evangelistic events are no exception to this rule. Here are some of the pros and cons of event evangelism:

Advantages

1. Special events help the church project a high profile in the community. These events give people the impression that your church is active and innovative.

2. Special events draw the lost and unchurched through curiosity. When your church sponsors special events, some folks will come because they want to know what is happening.

3. Special events cater to today's society. People enjoy things that are new, different, and exciting.

4. Special events generally require only a brief commitment from volunteers. This fact will help you enlist workers, and it makes it possible for some to participate who cannot do so on a regular basis.

5. Special events enable your members to express their imagination and creativity.

Disadvantages

1. Special events are just that—special. They are outside the realm of the church's usual evangelism program. It is easy to come to depend on special events for outreach and to neglect regular, ongoing activities. Many churches only do evangelism during their revivals each year. In these situations, evangelism itself becomes the exception rather than the norm.

2. Special events can be very expensive. A concert may be a great way to attract guests to your church, but a one-night concert might cost thousands of dollars. Special events also require a great expenditure of time and energy.

3. Special events may encourage some to participate, but they may also discourage others from getting involved.

4. Special events may produce lots of "decisions," but these decisions are notoriously hard to follow up, and it is often difficult to demonstrate lasting results.

5. Special events may produce a feeling that the next event must be bigger and better. It may be difficult to sponsor exciting and effective events year after year.[3]

As you can see, special evangelistic events have their good and bad points. Are they worth the effort? I believe they are. It is easy for churches to slip into a rut and do the same old things year after year. Sponsoring special events will help you avoid ruts and will enable you to reach people you could not touch otherwise.

REVIVAL MEETINGS

Revival meetings have been so common in the past that they hardly seem special. However, many churches become so burned out on revivals that they quit having them. Perhaps it is time to take a new look at an old method. The Billy Graham School of The Southern Baptist Theological Seminary surveyed effective evangelistic churches in the Southern Baptist Convention and discovered that almost half of the churches conduct revivals every year. These churches view revivals as a major evangelistic method. One pastor wrote:

> I have heard for many years that revivals are "on their way out!" During these years our church has continued to reach people for Christ through revivals. We consistently are among the ten leading churches in our state in baptisms. I hope we never learn that revivals are dead.[4]

Revival Preparation

There are many things to do to prepare for a revival. It is certainly true that thorough preparation is no substitute for the movement of the Holy Spirit, but on the other hand, God seems to bless hard work and careful preparation. I have participated in both well-prepared and ill-prepared meetings, and I saw a difference in the results every time. Here, then, are some pointers for good revival preparation.

Determine the purpose of the meeting. When I'm asked to preach in a revival meeting, I usually ask, "What is the purpose of the meeting?" This question usually prompts a lot of confusion. Often the pastor will ask what I mean. I reply, "Do you want to see your church members spiritually revived or the lost saved?" Almost always the pastor will answer, "Both." This is not surprising; both results are desirable. However, it is hard to accomplish both goals in the same meeting. Sermons on spiritual renewal are very different from evangelistic messages.

I am using the term *revival* improperly. A true revival is an outpouring of God's Spirit on believers. For someone to be "revived," that person must have been alive before. Thus, a true revival is not an experience for the unsaved; rather, it is a group experience for Christians. Most revival meetings prove ineffective because the church has not determined a clear purpose. In my opinion, a church does well to decide whether to have an evangelistic meeting or a revival meeting. The two are not the same.

Schedule the meeting. Scheduling has a lot to do with the success or failure of a meeting. Comedians say timing is everything, and the same holds true for revivals. Before scheduling your revival, consult with school and community leaders to see if anything will be happening in your community during the week you have in mind. Also, be careful to schedule the time of meeting appropriately. If you want parents with young children to attend, you will have to hold the services at an early hour.

Scheduling also involves the length of the meeting. When I was a boy, revivals often lasted two weeks. Later, meetings ran for one week. Nowadays, many churches plan four-day revivals. Consult with the lay leaders of your church to determine the best length for your congregation.

Invite competent personnel. If you want to secure a good preacher and good musicians for your meeting, you will have to invite them well in advance. Many full-time (or vocational) evangelists schedule their meetings two years in advance. Certainly, you should expect to invite your leaders at least a year ahead of time. If you are uncertain about whom to invite, you may want to consult with other pastors and the evangelism director of your state convention for their recommendations.

I have heard pastors discuss the advantages of inviting another pastor or a vocational evangelist to be the preacher. Obviously, pastors and evangelists can serve well and both are frequently used. However, I believe it is important to use vocational evangelists regularly. These men have the spiritual gift of evangelism, and they know how to conduct an effective meeting. Pastors should not let the excesses of a few rob them of the services of many gifted evangelists.

Budget for the meeting. Financial planning can affect your meeting either positively or negatively. I suggest that you include the following revival expenses in your annual church budget: publicity, travel, and hospitality for the evangelist and musician; and, activities during the meeting. For example, if you plan to have a youth pizza supper during the meeting, budget funds for that. The evangelist's travel and hotel expenses should be borne by the church. They should not be subtracted from the love offering given to the evangelist and musician. Some churches budget the love offering given to the evangelists. That is fine; however, you must clarify all this when you contact the evangelist. You should also be prepared to pay the evangelist at the end of the meeting.

Organize committees to prepare for and conduct the meeting. The more people you involve in revival preparation, the better. The Home Mission Board of the Southern Baptist Convention suggests the appointment of the following revival committees:

- Prayer Committee
- Publicity Committee
- Attendance Committee
- Hospitality Committee
- Music Committee
- Ushers Committee
- Prospects Committee
- Special Events Committee
- Counseling Committee.[5]

Of course, the work of committees is no substitute for the work of the Holy Spirit. Methods cannot replace the Spirit's power, but well-organized and functioning committees can help the meeting run smoothly and minimize distractions and foul-ups. Committees ought to be chosen by eight weeks before the meeting begins, and should start working intensively six weeks before the meeting. Most vocational evangelists have prepared materials to guide a church in preparing for a revival.[6]

Train counselors to help with the invitation. It is impossible to predict how many people will respond to the invitations during a revival meeting. Nevertheless, it is wise to be prepared for a good response. Well-trained invitation counselors free up the pastor to receive the people who come forward. Everyone making a decision can speak with the pastor who then directs each person to a counselor. Serving as counselors involves members in witnessing, and they become part of a growing number of trained and experienced soul winners in the church. These counselors can continue to help with the invitation time every Sunday.[7]

Visit evangelistic prospects before and during the meeting. A church revival should be an evangelistic harvesttime, a time when many people respond to the witness of the church members and the call of the Holy Spirit to be saved. During the six-week preparation period for the revival, focus your visitation and outreach efforts on witnessing to unsaved persons. The church staff and lay leaders should set aside extra time before and during the revival for evangelistic visitation.

Advertise the revival services. People do not attend revivals as much as they did in the past. In former times the revival was the best show in town, but this is no longer true. One older pastor asked, "Why don't we see a hundred people saved in a revival meeting like we used to?" I gave him a simple answer: "A hundred lost people don't attend the services anymore." Though fewer unchurched people may attend, they certainly cannot come if they do not know about the meeting. Be sure the news of your meeting is spread all over your community. Newspaper ads, radio announcements, handbills, posters, and yard signs should all be used to announce the meeting.

Pray for the revival meeting. The Prayer Committee is the most important committee. You should see to it that your church's prayer warriors serve on this committee. Ask them to pray for prospects, for the evangelists, and for the church. Their prayers serve as the propellant to fuel the revival.

Plan special nights. Special nights or special events provide opportunities to increase enthusiasm and attendance. Your church can choose from a number of different special emphases. Some of the more common include: youth night, children's night, Sunday school night, friends' night, a concert, pack-the-pew, seniors' night, and neighbors' night. You should plan a special emphasis for every night of the meeting.

Prepare for follow-up. It is important to prepare both a plan and personnel for follow-up. Those who make decisions for Christ will need tender loving care by people who are trained to provide it. We will learn more about this in the next chapter.[8]

When the Billy Graham School asked evangelistic pastors about the keys to a successful revival, they mentioned these three keys most often. First, their churches plan and prepare extensively for each meeting. Second, their churches emphasize prayer. One church spends the entire week before revival in prayer and fasting. Another church maintains a day-round prayer vigil during the meeting. For these churches, preparation and prayer go hand in hand. Third, most of their churches invite a vocational evangelist to lead the meetings. Al Jackson, pastor of the rapidly growing Lakeview Baptist Church in Auburn, Alabama, said, "We usually use a full-time vocational evangelist to lead our revival services. Though we have experienced some good revivals with other men, we have found that a full-time evangelist is gifted by God to draw the net."[9]

Conducting the Evangelistic Meeting

The way an evangelistic meeting is conducted will vary according to the time and place and circumstances. Obviously, an open-air meeting at the local football field will call for different preparations than a meeting being held at a local church building. Still, there are some common denominators in all situations:

1. *Check out the physical arrangements.* It is important to check out the lighting, seating, and sound system. If you are planning an outdoor meeting, be sure to provide an alternate site in case of bad weather.

2. *Schedule prayer meetings before the service.* Ask your Prayer Committee to plan these. Some churches conduct prayer meetings during the services as well.

3. *Visit the lost and unchurched during the week before the meeting.*

4. *Ask the evangelist to meet with the youth and older children during the meeting.* He can make an appropriate evangelistic appeal to both groups.

5. *Keep announcements short and to the point.* This is not the time to share the plans for Vacation Bible School or the Brotherhood fish fry. Confine announcements to those pertaining to the revival.

6. *Use heart-warming music.* All congregations need to learn new hymns, but a revival is not the time and place for that. The music should be chosen for its evangelistic impact.

7. *Get information about guests who attend the service.*

8. *Plan the invitation time.* The evangelist, musicians, and pastor should be clear on what will happen during the invitation time. Normally the evangelist begins the invitation, and the pastor stands at the front of the church to receive those who make decisions. Usually, the evangelist turns the invitation over to the pastor at some point. The pastor continues or ends the invitation as led by the Holy Spirit. The pastor should not "repreach" the evangelist's sermon.

9. *Explain the love offering carefully.* If the church takes up a love offering for the evangelist and musician, the pastor should explain the purpose for the offering.

Many churches still sponsor revivals, but they are taking on a new format. Some churches are holding revival weekends (Friday through Sunday meetings). Other churches are conducting one-day meetings. Still others have chosen to conduct revival services every Sunday for a month. Another approach is to have a different speaker every night, and some churches conduct youth revivals. I suggest that churches experiment to find what works best for them. Innovation may breathe new life into an old evangelistic method.

SPECIAL EVANGELISTIC EVENTS

Description

Thad Hamilton describes special evangelistic events as "innovative evangelistic events conducted in church facilities and public areas." These events are quite varied, and may include holiday festivals, concerts, pageants, banquets, meals, dramas, sports clinics, block parties, street meetings, and felt-need seminars. Hamilton illustrates these special events with the following acrostic:

Exciting
Vitality
Equipping
New
Tailor-made
Soul-winning[10]

Special events are exciting because they bring new people into the church. They represent a change from the ordinary, and help to prevent churches from falling into a rut. Special events inject vitality into a church. Special events show your community that your congregation is lively and involved. Special events equip members for service. They give members the opportunity to discover, develop, and employ their talents and gifts for the Lord. Special events are new and they are different. Their novelty helps make them attractive. Special events can be tailor-made or customized to fit a particular church's situation. Finally, the bottom-line purpose for all special events is soul-winning, to bring people to Christ.[11]

Rationale

The Saddleback Community Church in Orange County, California, uses many "bridge events" to touch the surrounding community. Most of these events are conducted annually on a community-wide basis. They call these "bridge events" because they "are designed to build a bridge between our church and our community." Many of these events are major productions, designed to capture the attention and interest of the community. They include a Harvest Party (at Halloween), Christmas Eve services, Easter services, Western Day (near the Fourth of July), as well as other seasonal celebrations, concerts, and productions. Pastor Rick Warren says, "Some of our bridge events are overtly evangelistic while others we consider 'pre-evangelism'—they simply make the unchurched in our community aware of our church."[12]

Principles of Planning

Advance planning is the key to success. This statement is true in most areas of life, but it is especially true in regard to special evangelistic events. As you dream and then plan to fulfill those dreams, you will want to follow these principles:

1. *Define the target audience.* Ask yourself this question: Who do we want to reach through this event? Obviously, a program designed to reach young people will be designed differently than a program to reach senior citizens. Some events might attract a broad spectrum of people, while others target a specific audience. Determine your target group in the earliest stages of planning.

2. *Publicize the event.* People can't attend the event if they don't know about it. You can't use too much publicity. Buy some advertising and plead for free advertising. The more you advertise your event, the more impressed the community will be.

3. *Plan the event carefully.* Try to anticipate everything that can go wrong. Murphy's Law–"Anything that can go wrong will go wrong"–unfortunately applies to evangelistic events. Think about security, medical care, parking, special permits, seating, sound systems, sanitation facilities, and traffic control. A Louisville church sponsored a major holiday event, hoping one thousand people would attend. When ten thousand people arrived, a big traffic jam occurred. The police were not amused, and they insisted on prior notice for any future events. You will want to be sure that your liability insurance covers the event, especially if it is held away from the church campus. If you are borrowing the idea for an event from another church, ask for advice. You will probably be given some good insight about things to do and pitfalls to avoid.

4. *Determine your purpose.* What do you want this event to do for your church? The event should have one primary purpose. Clarifying the purpose will aid your planning. Rick Warren stated that some events his church sponsors are deliberately evangelistic, while others are pre-evangelistic (get acquainted with our church) events. If you plan to give an invitation during the program, you will need trained counselors standing by.

5. *Conduct the event efficiently.* If it is worth doing, it is worth doing well. Unchurched people will judge your church by the

quality of the event. You would do better to hold one quality event than to sponsor two mediocre productions. You don't want the people to leave frustrated or disappointed.

6. *Plan for effective follow-up.* If you hope to obtain additional prospects for your church, you will need to devise a way to get the attenders' names and addresses. If you hold the event away from your church facilities, be sure the people learn where your church is located. Give literature about becoming a Christian and about your church to everyone who attends. It is also important to have people trained and ready to call and visit potential prospects. Don't neglect the follow-up. Often, the event takes so much time and energy that church members are exhausted when it is over. They rest for a few days, and then someone says, "What have we done about the people who filled out response cards?" If you want your event to really help your church grow, you will need to plan for immediate follow-up.

7. *Evaluate the results.* After the event you will want to bring the key workers together for an evaluation meeting. The meeting gives you an opportunity to learn what went well and what did not. This information will enable you to do a better job next time. A follow-up meeting also gives you an opportunity to praise and affirm those who worked hard to make the event happen.[13]

SUMMARY

There are many different special evangelistic events your church can use to reach people for Christ. Special events can generate excitement in your congregation and attract attention in the community. On the downside, special events are often costly and time-consuming. Some churches find that they receive little evangelistic benefit from these events. Other churches, especially large ones, see special events as a vital part of their outreach program.

Revivals and evangelistic meetings are probably the most common type of special event. The keys to a successful revival are prayer, planning, and preparation. Some churches that got burned out on revivals are returning to this method, though they may use a different format.

Creativity and careful planning will help ensure that other special events have their desired effect. True, special events have advantages and disadvantages. However, it seems to me that they are worth the trouble. Many churches get into a rut. The same old programs may not touch unchurched people in the community. Churches need to do something out of the ordinary. If nothing else, these special events will let your community know that your church is still alive.

STUDY QUESTIONS

1. What are the advantages and disadvantages of special events?
2. What is the difference between a revival and an evangelistic meeting?
3. Why is it important to determine the purpose of the event?
4. What are two special events your church might sponsor?
5. Why is it important to conduct some kind of special event periodically?

FOR FURTHER STUDY

Hamilton, Thad. *Special Evangelist Events*. Atlanta: Home Mission Board, 1994.

Harris, Richard. *Revival Planbook for the Local Church*. Atlanta: Home Mission Board, 1993.

Huston, Sterling W. *Crusade Evangelism and the Local Church*. Minneapolis: World Wide Publications, 1984.

Lewis, Larry L. *Organize to Evangelize*. Nashville: Broadman Press, 1988.

Wicker, Dale. "Practical Ideas for Event Evangelism," *Growing Churches* (April-June 1992): 60–61.

CHAPTER 14

RETAIN AND ASSIMILATE THE CONVERTS

Since I teach at a seminary, I know lots of young couples. Often they bring their newborn babies for me to admire. As a veteran father, I know that these new parents have a big job ahead of them. Now that they've had a baby, they have to raise her. Having a baby is not just an event. It is the beginning of a long process.

In the Great Commission (Matt. 28:18–20) Jesus commanded his followers to "make disciples" of all the people in the world. There is a big difference between a convert and a disciple. A disciple is a mature believer who is capable of reproducing. Evangelism, then, is a process that is not complete until the evangelized becomes an evangelist. In this chapter we will discuss ways to help new converts in Christ grow and develop until they are able to function as mature Christians. Discipling new converts and assimilating them into the church is the second phase of effective evangelism.

THE IMPORTANCE OF RETENTION

Studies of church membership statistics show the need for retaining new members. A study of Southern Baptist churches revealed that 29 percent of resident members are inactive.[1] That figure does not include nonresident church members. *Nonresident* member is a Southern Baptist euphemism for misplaced members. These people's names are still on church rolls, but the churches do not know where they are.

Methodist statistics are no better. John Savage conducted a study of the United Methodist Church and found that 33 percent of its members were inactive.[2] A recent study by Robert Jeamby found that Presbyterian churches lose half of their new members within two years. Why do churches lose so many members? Jeamby identified three primary reasons for the loss of church members:

- *Failed expectations.* Often the church, and especially the pastor, did not meet the expectations of the new members. The church failed to provide the services and relationships the new members desired.

- *Nonacceptance and unrelatedness.* Others interviewed mentioned a lack of acceptance by the congregation, so these dropouts never really connected with the church.

- *Lifestyle and work schedule conflicts.* Some said they could not attend worship because of their work schedules. Others found the lifestyle of the church members to be incompatible with their own.[3]

James Hightower lists several primary reasons why people leave a church:

- Personal and family crises
- Life transitions
- Shift of priorities
- Interpersonal conflicts
- Burnout
- Immoral behavior
- Problems with church leaders
- Church conflict
- Move to another community.[4]

Clearly, churches cannot prevent some of these problems. If a corporation transfers your best deacon to another city, there is not much you can do. However, the church can deal with many of the crises listed above.

Beyond the problem of church dropouts is the problem of unproductive church members. Many church members never mature in their faith and never become productive Christians. They may attend services occasionally, but they really do nothing for the church other than fill a pew. Roland Q. Leavell estimated that:

- 20 percent never pray
- 25 percent never read the Bible
- 30 percent never attend church
- 40 percent never give to any cause
- 50 percent never go to Sunday school
- 60 percent never attend evening services
- 70 percent never give to missions
- 80 percent never go to prayer meeting
- 90 percent never have family worship
- 95 percent never win a soul to Christ.[5]

Leavell wrote these words in 1942. The percentages are probably even worse today. What can be done about these vexing problems? The answer is to develop a program through which new converts get a good start in their Christian lives.

THE NEEDS OF NEW BELIEVERS

As you begin to work with new believers, it is helpful to clarify the goal of follow-up. All pastors want their members to be "conformed to the likeness of his Son" (Rom. 8:29). God wants these people to become like Jesus. That is God's purpose for them, and it should be your purpose as well. Simply put, a disciple is one who learns from Christ and imitates him. The Gospel of John describes a disciple in three ways. First, a disciple studies the Bible continually (John 8:31). Second, a disciple loves and sacrifices for others (John 13:34–35). Third, a disciple abides with Christ and bears fruit for Christ (John 15:4–5).[6]

The process of helping spiritual infants become like Christ is called *discipling*. It could just as well be described as spiritual pediatrics. You won't accomplish this task in two weeks, but you will find great joy in watching new Christians grow in their faith. Fortunately, you are not alone in this. The Holy Spirit works in the lives of the new believers to make them more like Christ every day. Theologians call this process "sanctification." It simply means that the Holy Spirit works in believers to make them like Christ. This process is progressive, not instantaneous. Thus, disciplers need to be patient and give the Holy Spirit time to work in lives of converts.

I can testify from personal experience that newborn babies need a lot of care. They can't feed, bathe, or dress themselves. They can't walk or talk. They depend on their parents for everything. Newborn Christians are much the same. They don't know how to talk—they've not yet learned to pray. They don't know how to walk—they don't know biblical ethics. They don't know how to bathe—they don't know about confession. And, they don't know how to feed themselves—they haven't learned how to study the Bible yet. But, so often when a person professes Christ as Savior, we shake her hand, pat her on the back, and wish her well in the Christian life. If we patted a newborn baby on the head, wished her a happy life, and walked away, we would be criminally negligent. In the same way, abandoning spiritual infants is criminal.

New Christians have many needs. Perhaps their greatest and most immediate need is for *assurance.* After people accept Christ as Savior, they are prone to question or doubt their salvation. The discipler can provide great help here by assuring the new believer that such doubts are normal and by sharing comforting verses like Romans 10:13 and John 10:28.

New believers also need *love* (John 15:12). Psychologists have discovered that newborn babies need to feel love and security. This early bonding makes for a healthy personality. The discipler can provide this bonding by spending time with the new Christian and by giving lots of tender loving care.

Young Christians need *nourishment* (1 Pet. 2:2). Babes in Christ cannot feed themselves. They need someone to show them how to study the Bible so they can receive spiritual food. Many new believers don't even know how to find a biblical text. This is where the discipler can help. By teaching basic Bible study methods and principles of interpretation, the discipler can teach the new convert to feed himself.

Like all babies, new believers need *protection* (1 Pet. 5:8). New believers struggle with the "world, the flesh, and the devil" just as all Christians do. However, new believers are less able to protect themselves. The discipler should teach the convert basic survival techniques like a daily devotional time and Scripture memorization. Jesus resisted temptation by quoting Scripture verses. This method will work for new believers as well, but they must be encouraged and taught to memorize Scripture.

Finally, new Christians need *training* (Acts 2:42). New believers need to learn doctrine, ethics, biblical backgrounds, and lots of other things. The discipler will teach the new believer these things and more. Some teaching will take place through reading and oral instruction. However, much teaching will take place as a result of the personal example of the discipler.[7]

METHODS OF FOLLOW-UP

Waylon Moore's book *New Testament Follow-Up* is an excellent guide for those who want to help new believers. Moore explains the four methods of follow-up found in the New Testament.

Four Ways to Follow Up

Personal contact. This is the "with" principle. It is essential for the discipler to be with the convert (Mark 3:14). Jesus called his disciples to be with him and learn from him. Jesus spent three years training his disciples and preparing them for their ministry. Paul invited Timothy to go with him and learn to be a missionary. Through frequent contact with your disciple, you can share your life and pour yourself into the new believer. This contact should be regular and intentional. If you develop a plan for discipleship, you will see your disciple grow more quickly.

Personal prayer. Jesus spent much time praying for his disciples. Paul's epistles show that he did the same. Similarly, disciplers should pray for their disciples every day. These intercessory prayers will erect a protective wall around the disciples. The practice of intercessory prayer will also set an example for the new believer.

Personal representatives. Paul's letters reveal the apostle's deep concern for the welfare of his disciples. When he could not visit with them personally, he sent a representative. At various times Paul sent Timothy, Titus, Tychicus, and Epaphroditus to minister to the new believers in his behalf. When modern disciplers are unable to meet with their disciples, they do well to follow Paul's example. We surely want our disciples to develop consistency in their Christian lives. One way we can achieve that is to ensure that they stay on their discipleship regimen, even if the primary discipler cannot meet with them.

Personal correspondence. Paul's letters to Timothy, Titus, and Philemon are good examples of personal correspondence. Paul wrote to his disciples to encourage them in their Christian walk and service. If we are separated from our disciples, we can correspond with them to demonstrate our concern and to communicate vital truths. Letters are especially effective as a ministry to college students and military personnel. In modern times it is possible to communicate by phone, fax, and E-mail. The point here is to communicate in some way.[8]

The Qualities of a Good Discipler

Some members in the church will be more suited than others for the ministry of discipling. Often they are not the people who are the best evangelists. As you seek disciplers, look for members who demonstrate these qualities in their lives:

- They have servant hearts.
- They seek ways to help others.
- They are willing to give time to discipling.
- They show the fruit of the Spirit in their lives.
- They know and use their spiritual gifts.
- They can set a good example for new believers.
- They can be patient with young Christians.
- They have developed good spiritual habits.[9]

In his "Mentoring Mandate Seminar," Waylon Moore offers these pointers for disciplers:

- Daily mentoring is much more effective than weekly mentoring, especially in the convert's first weeks of discipleship.
- Begin working with the convert within forty-eight hours of his profession of faith.
- Give the disciple total and unconditional love. Just like human babies, spiritual babies make big messes, and the discipler must love them a lot to clean them up.
- Involve the disciples in sharing their salvation testimony as soon as possible. This helps them develop a pattern of witnessing from the beginning.

The Pastor's Role in Follow-up

Lay people will (and should) do most of the follow-up ministry, but the pastor also plays an important role.

- The pastor serves as a role model for new Christians (1 Pet. 5:3). Naturally they will look up to their pastor. His example in personal devotions and Christian living will influence the new believers.

- The pastor must consciously and carefully teach spiritual truth in a way that young Christians can comprehend.[10]

- The pastor must see to it that every new member is discipled. A layperson or staff member may supervise the ministry of follow-up, but the pastor must ascertain that it is done and done right. In the beginning of the ministry, the pastor may need to train the disciplers and provide them with appropriate materials.[11]

ASSIMILATING NEW MEMBERS

Many churches have a "back door" problem. People come in through the front door, accepting Christ and joining the church, but they soon leave the church by way of the back door. It takes so much time, money, and effort to reach people for Christ; it is a shame to lose them through neglect.

What are the keys to retaining new members? Basically, they need two things: a sense of belonging and a sense of involvement. In other words, we need to make new members feel accepted, and we need to get them involved in a meaningful way in the church. Lyle Schaller has written that "at least one-third, and perhaps as many as one-half, of all Protestant church members do not feel a sense of belonging to the congregation. . . . They have been received into membership, but have never felt they have been accepted into the fellowship circle."[12] Small wonder then that so many members drop out.

Follow-up workers can help new Christians feel loved and accepted into the church fellowship. Who will fulfill these responsibilities for those who join your church by transfer of membership from another congregation? There are many different responses to this need, many of which are complementary.

Sponsors for New Members

One of the most common approaches to assimilating new members is to assign them sponsors. Some churches call this "The Adoption Plan," while other churches call this the "Big Brother/Big Sister Plan." "The Encourager Plan" assigns each new member to an "Encourager," who fulfills these responsibilities:[13]

- Contacts the new member when he or she joins the church.
- Contacts the new member weekly for at least three months.
- Escorts the new member to Sunday school.
- Sits with the new member in worship services.
- Takes the new member on a tour of the building.
- Introduces the new member to other church members.
- Introduces the new member to church staff and lay leaders.
- Interprets church jargon and traditions for the new member.
- Prays for the new member.

You can readily see the advantages of this plan. Pleasant View Baptist Church in Lincoln County, Kentucky, adopted this plan and trained forty-two Encouragers. Pastor Vola Brown says this plan "gives a more personal touch" than the traditional new members' class the church had offered before.[14]

The Pastor's Ministry to New Members

New members need to develop a healthy relationship with their pastor. They need to feel the pastor's love and support. Pastors can minister to new members in several ways.

1. Pastors can minister to the new members through sermons. Pastors do well to keep new members in mind as they prepare their sermons.

2. Pastors can write encouraging letters.

3. Pastors can see to it that all new members each have a sponsor and/or participate in a new members' class.

4. Pastors can answer new members' questions.

5. Pastors can become well acquainted with new members. Many pastors make a point of visiting with new members in their homes.

During this visit the pastor can ask questions like these:

ANSWERING QUESTIONS

The questions of new Christians will vary from person to person, but Rick Warren believes all new members want to know the answers to these questions, even if the questions remain unspoken.

- Do I fit in here?
- Will the people accept me?
- Does anybody here want to know me?
- Will anyone befriend me?
- Am I needed?
- Can I make a contribution to this church?
- What are the advantages of joining this church?
- What is required of members?
- What do they expect of me?[15]

- Who are the members of the household?
- Are there lost or unchurched persons in the family?
- What factors led the new member to join the church?
- What does the member hope to receive from the church?
- What does the member hope to contribute?
- Does the member have any talents or skills that might help the church?
- What is the member's educational and work experience?
- Does the member have any major problems?
- What are the member's interests and hobbies?
- Who should be contacted in case of an emergency?

It is good for pastors to keep a notebook with such information about each family in the church. If you move to another church, you can leave the notebook for the next pastor. I'm sure the new pastor will be glad to get it.

New Members' Class

Many churches offer classes for new members. In some churches the class is optional. In others, the class is required. Rick Warren believes very strongly that the class should be a requirement for membership. He says, "The *manner* in which people join your church will determine their effectiveness as members for years to come." He identifies the new members' class as the most important class in the church "because it sets the tone and expectation level for everything else that follows. The very best time to elicit a strong commitment from your members is at the moment they join. If little is required to join, very little can be expected from your members later on." For Warren, the membership class spells the difference between a weak congregation or a strong congregation.[16]

I think it is advantageous for the pastor to teach the class, or at least part of it, because it gives the pastor an opportunity to get to know the new members better.

The new members' class is important. Its purpose is to help new members:

- To strengthen their Christian commitment
- To understand what their church expects of them
- To be aware of their new church's programs, activities, and ministries
- To understand their church's purpose and history
- To find a place of service in the congregation
- To understand Christian doctrine and ethics

Different churches have different formats for the class. The First Baptist Church of Augusta, Georgia, used this five-lesson format:

1. Your Growth as a Christian
2. Using Your Bible
3. Your Church's Organization and Covenant
4. Your Church's Beliefs
5. Sharing Your Faith

Saddleback Community Church requires new members to participate in a four-hour session called "Discovering Saddleback Membership." Different groups are offered for children, youth, and adults. This is the outline for the course:

I. Our Salvation
   A. Making sure you are a Christian
   B. The symbols of salvation
      1. Baptism
      2. Communion
II. Our Statements
   A. Our Purpose Statement: Why we exist
   B. Our Vision Statement: What we intend to do
   C. Our Faith Statement: What we believe
   D. Our Values Statement: What we practice
III. Our Strategy
   A. Brief history of Saddleback
   B. Who we are trying to reach (our target)
   C. Our Life Development Process to help you grow
   D. The S.A.D.D.L.E.B.A.C.K. strategy
IV. Our Structure
   A. How our church is structured for growth
   B. Our affiliation
   C. What it means to be a member
   D. What is my next step after joining?[17]

A New Members' Banquet

Many churches sponsor a banquet for their new members every quarter or even every month. They provide this banquet at no charge to their new members. This gathering gives new members a chance to meet the church staff and lay leaders. It also makes the new members feel welcome and appreciated.

Church Membership Covenant

Church covenants are certainly not new.[18] Churches have used them for centuries, but many churches are now emphasizing the church covenant in new and more meaningful ways. These churches typically write their own covenant rather than using a standard covenant from a church manual. When a person joins the church, that person is required to sign the covenant and promise to live by its requirements. In addition, the whole congregation renews its commitment to the covenant each year on the church's anniversary. You can readily discern the advantages to using the covenant as these churches do. This covenant helps to ensure that your new members are serious about their church commitment. It also serves to remind all the members of their previous church commitments.

Involvement in a Small Group

As mentioned earlier, new members need to feel a sense of belonging. This can best be achieved through a small group. The small group may be a Sunday school class, a cell group, or another small group connected with the church. Many churches automatically enroll all new members in an appropriate Sunday school class. Others ask them to join a discipleship group or home Bible study. The main thing here is to be sure they participate in a group with face-to-face fellowship.

Integrated Approach

Many growing churches have adopted an integrated approach to assimilation. That is, they use several different methods to assimilate new members into the life of the church. For example, the Rock Springs Baptist Church in Easley, South Carolina, is a growing, traditional church. Sunday school attendance has grown from 260 in 1983 to 863 in 1994. This church encourages all new members to attend a nine-week, new members' class that gives an orientation to the church and presents studies of salvation, spiritual gifts, and other Christian doctrine. During the class the new members have a chance to meet the staff. The church sponsors a new members' fellowship every quarter. Finally, the staff assigns a sponsor to each new church member. The sponsors provide orientation, support, and visitation for two months.

First Baptist Church of Leesburg, Florida, also uses an integrated approach. The philosophy of this church is expressed in the following quote: "Studies reveal that infants require early bonding to develop properly. For this reason, they need to be held, cuddled, and talked to. New believers also need time to bond with their church family."[19] When a person makes a profession of faith, the church gives the person a copy of "Welcome to God's Family," a tract for new Christians. Then the church assigns an encourager to the new Christian. The encourager leads the convert through the booklet, *Survival Kit for New Christians.* The church also enrolls all new members in Sunday school so they will experience small-group interaction.

All new members at First Baptist Church participate in an orientation seminar. Then they participate in a series of discipleship courses. New Christians enroll in "Beginning Your Christian Walk." Those who have finished this first course can go on to "Maturing in Your Christian Walk." The next level of training is called "Serving Christ in the World." Courses at this level include: "Discovering Your Place of Service in the First Family," "Defending Your Faith," "Advanced Witness Training," "Counseling Basics," and "Spiritual Gifts Seminar." Through these courses the church tries to place every new member in a ministry position.[20]

Involvement in Ministry

As mentioned above, new members need a sense of belonging and involvement. In order to help new members get involved, churches like First Baptist Church of Leesburg help them discover their spiritual gifts and provide them with ministry training. These efforts help new members find fulfilling and satisfying places of service both within and outside the church. Several spiritual gift inventories are available that you can use to help both new and old members discover their spiritual gifts. In addition, it is a good idea to ask every new member to fill out a talent survey form. This provides new members with opportunities to use their talents and experience for the Lord, and it will help you find the workers you need for various programs and projects.

SUMMARY

Most churches struggle to close the back door. They may reach some people for Christ, but they find that many new members do not remain long. Neither do they assume ministry responsibilities. The solution to this frustrating problem is proper follow-up and assimilation. New converts need lots of attention just as new babies do. Churches need to be sensitive to this need and to train follow-up workers to guide new Christians in their new faith. These converts also need to be assimilated into the life of the church. New members need to feel a sense of belonging and involvement. Churches can help with this by providing encouragers, new members' classes, banquets, seminars, and small-group involvement. The main thing here is to develop a specific plan administered by a specific person. We dare not let these new Christians slip through the cracks.

STUDY QUESTIONS

1. What is the "back door" problem?
2. What are the two primary needs of new members?
3. What qualities should disciplers possess?
4. What are four methods churches can use to meet the needs of new members?
5. What is the pastor's role in assimilating new members?

FOR FURTHER STUDY

Hightower, James. *After They Join*. Nashville: Convention Press, 1995.

McIntosh, Gary and Glen Martin. *Finding Them, Keeping Them*. Nashville: Broadman Press, 1992.

Moore, Waylon B. *Multiplying Disciples: The New Testament Method for Church Growth*. Tampa: Missions Unlimited, 1981.

Moore, Waylon B. *New Testament Follow-Up*. Grand Rapids: Eerdmans Publishing Co., 1963.

Schaller, Lyle E. *Assimilating New Members*. Nashville: Abingdon Press, 1978.

Warren, Rick. *The Purpose Driven Church*. Grand Rapids: Zondervan Publishing House, 1995.

CHAPTER 15

PLANT NEW CHURCHES

➤ ———————— ⬥

You may be surprised that I have included a chapter on church planting in a book on church evangelism. Most people think of church planting as a missions activity, not an evangelistic activity. This notion is both mistaken and unfortunate. Peter Wagner has boldly stated that church planting is "the single most effective evangelistic method under heaven."[1] It may well be that the best evangelistic method you could employ in your community is to plant a new church. I hope you recall the four types of church growth mentioned in chapter 2: internal growth, expansion growth, extension growth, and cross-cultural growth. Church planting is basically extension growth. In this chapter you will learn why church planting is important and how to do it.

WHY PLANT NEW CHURCHES?

There are many reasons why existing churches should plant new churches. I will list a few of them here:

1. *Church planting is biblical.* Though the term *church planting* is not used in the New Testament, the New Testament writers often mentioned the practice. Luke used much of his Acts narrative in describing Paul's efforts at church planting. Paul tried to start churches everywhere he went. His success is evident, not only in Acts but also in letters he wrote to the young churches. Paul

was not content to just make converts; he remained in each city until a congregation had been established.

2. *New churches win more people to Christ.* Church growth research shows that new churches have a higher conversion rate than older churches. When church growth researchers studied all the Protestant churches in the Santa Clarita Valley of California, they discovered that older churches were baptizing 4 persons for every 100 members, while newer churches were baptizing 16 persons for every 100 members. The Southern Baptist Home Mission Board reports that new Anglo churches baptized 13 persons per 100 members, while older churches baptized 3 persons per 100 members.[2]

3. *New churches grow more rapidly than older churches.* Kirk Hadaway's research has revealed that new Southern Baptist churches are more likely to grow than older churches. The same thing proved true among American Baptists, Presbyterians, and the United Church of Christ.[3] Why are newer churches more likely to grow than older churches?

   • New churches are more flexible and open to change.

   • New churches welcome new members. Older churches tend to become closed social groups that do not welcome new members. In newer churches the friendship networks have not yet solidified and the members are more accepting of new people.

   • New churches are naturally more volatile than older organizations. New organizations are more likely to grow or die.[4]

4. *New churches are needed to replace dying churches.* Churches, like people, go through a life cycle of birth, growth, maturity, decline, and death. Eighty percent of America's 350,000 churches are either plateaued or declining, reports Win Arn. He believes that 80 to 85 percent of these churches are in the declining stage. Beyond that, 3,500 to 4,000 churches die each year.[5] Obviously, these churches must be replaced or communities will be unchurched and lost people unreached.

5. *New churches are needed to reach new generations.* Most churches want to reach people of all age groups; however, few are willing to change in order to do so. Church growth teachers often

say, "We need new churches to reach new generations." All generations—preboomers, baby boomers, and baby busters—have different expectations about how to do church. It is difficult for one church to meet their diverse needs and expectations. Few churches can be all things to all people, but new churches can target population groups for ministry.

6. *New churches are needed for new communities.* If you visit any city in North America, you will find new suburbs and new housing developments. These new communities need churches. Wise denominations track development in their cities and plant new churches.

7. *New churches are needed to reach various ethnic groups.* People need to hear the gospel in their own language. They need to worship in ways that are culturally satisfying to them. This outreach and worship can only be provided by new churches. Of course, we should welcome all types of people to our churches, but we will reach more of them through church extension than by church expansion.

8. *New churches are essential to denominational growth.* Growing denominations plant more new churches than declining denominations. Denominations grow when they work hard at planting churches. When they neglect church planting, they decline. Lyle Schaller says, "From a denominational perspective, one road to numerical growth is to organize more new missions. A reasonable goal is a number equal to at least 2 to 3 percent of the current number of congregations."[6]

OBJECTIONS TO CHURCH PLANTING

If church planting is so needful and important, why would anyone object? That is a good question, but surprisingly, many do object. Many objections are based on ignorance. Most pastors and lay leaders are unaware of the information presented above. Most seminaries do not offer a course in church planting; and where courses are offered, they are offered as electives. As a result, most pastors know little about church planting. Popular Christian magazines seldom publish stories about church planting. For this reason, most lay leaders seldom even think about church planting.

Here are some common objections to church planting:

1. *"We already have more than enough churches."* Some would even say there are too many churches. That might be true in a few places, but most areas need new churches. They do not need more churches of the same type, but they need new churches that can minister to groups of unchurched people. These areas may need a Hispanic church or a Korean church or a church for baby busters. Careful community surveys will reveal large numbers of unchurched people, even in communities with many churches. Many of these people live in multihousing units (apartments or mobile home parks). Only one of every twenty multihousing residents in the United States is a church member.

2. *"Church planting is too expensive."* Those who raise this objection are saying that their church cannot afford to sponsor a new mission. There is some validity to this objection. Some types of church planting are very expensive. If you must begin with a nice brick building and a full-time seminary-trained pastor, then church planting will be expensive. However, there are other ways to plant churches. The apostle Paul planted many churches without money. Charles Brock explains in his book, *Indigenous Church Planting,* how we can emulate Paul and start churches without incurring huge expenses.

3. *"It doesn't matter."* Many church members believe that everyone will ultimately be saved. These people see little or no need for church planting. If one does not believe non-Christians are lost and without hope in the world, then there is no motivation to give the money or put out the efforts required by church planting.

4. *"People in other churches will be offended."* Certainly, it is important to maintain good relations with other churches. However, when you show the members of these churches how many people in the community are unchurched, they may understand the need. Also, it is important to emphasize that the unchurched are your target group and to assure them that you have no intention of "stealing sheep." You should help them understand that new churches stimulate church attendance at existing churches. Rather than detract from older churches, new churches seem to boost church attendance in the entire community.

5. *"We don't know how to start a new church."* Almost every denomination has consultants who can advise churches on the steps to take. In addition, many good materials and conferences are available to provide guidance.

THE BENEFITS OF CHURCH PLANTING

Planting new churches brings many benefits to the sponsoring churches. In fact, the benefits are so numerous that I cannot list them all here. I have listed a few of the more obvious:

1. *New churches win more people to Christ.* According to one estimate, there are 170 million lost people in the United States. The most efficient way to win them to Christ is by planting churches. Another study found that 60 percent of the adults who join a new congregation were unchurched before joining.[7] Why are new congregations more evangelistic than old ones? New churches emphasize evangelism and organize the congregation's life around evangelism and outreach. Older churches tend to give more of their attention to the care of their members.

2. *Church planting makes us obedient servants of Christ.* In his Great Commission (Matt. 28:18–20), Jesus commanded us to make disciples of all the world's people by going to them, baptizing them, and teaching them his commands. The only way we can fulfill this commission is by planting churches.

3. *Church planting brings joy and satisfaction to the members of the new congregation and to the members of the sponsoring church.*

4. *Church planting stimulates growth in the mother church.* Some pastors hesitate to start a daughter church for fear that it will weaken the mother church. Actually, the opposite is true in the long run. The First Baptist Church of Arlington, Texas, began a church-planting project called Mission Arlington. This project took the gospel to apartment complexes all over the city. By 1994 more than 140 cell groups with 2,000 members met weekly to study the Bible and worship. When the project began in 1986, First Baptist averaged 1,200 in Sunday school; in 1994 the church averaged 1,800 under the leadership of the same pastor, Charles Wade. In 1980, when Rick Warren went to Orange County, California, to plant a new

church, he announced dual goals: to have a church of 20,000 members by the year 2020 and to start a new daughter congregation each year. In 1994 the Saddleback Valley Community Church averaged more than eight thousand in worship, and the church has started twenty-four daughter churches in fourteen years. Clearly, church planting does not hinder the mother church's growth.[8]

5. *Starting new churches gives more people opportunities to exercise church leadership.* Many Christians have spiritual gifts of leadership, but they hesitate to use them in older churches with entrenched leaders. New churches provide an avenue for these people to use their gifts.

6. *New churches stimulate the growth of denominations.* New church development is both a cause and a sign of denominational vitality. This was one firm conclusion expressed by David Roozen and Kirk Hadaway in their important book, *Church and Denominational Growth.* In this book they contrast the decline of mainline Protestant denominations with the growth of denominations like the Missouri Synod Lutherans, Assemblies of God, and the Southern Baptist Convention. The key difference between the declining and growing denominations was church-planting activity.

7. *Planting a new church helps a church to be extroverted.* Too many churches are introverted. The members are primarily concerned with maintaining their organization and ministering to each other. Churches like this may be efficient, but they are not effective. A healthy church is extroverted. The people form ministry opportunities outside the church's walls.

8. *Planting churches yields God's blessings.* Starting a new church takes time, money, and effort, but God blesses those who are obedient. One pastor told of sending the deacon who was the biggest giver in the church to help start a mission. The pastor said that even though the church's offerings suffered for about six months, at the end of two years the mother church's budget was twice as large as before. You can't outgive God. He will replace what you give away in his service.

CHURCH PLANTING MODELS

There are many different models of church planting. No approach is appropriate for every situation. Many factors will determine which model you should use and how you should use it. If God leads you to plant a church, learn all you can about church planting and pray that God will guide you in the work. The approaches listed below have proven successful in the past.

Core Group

A group of members from the mother church forms the nucleus of members at the mission. Sometimes these people volunteer, and sometimes the pastor or missions committee selects them. This approach has two advantages. First, the group is stable from the beginning. Often the core group includes musicians, Sunday school teachers, and a deacon or two. Thus the mission pastor does not have to struggle to discover and train individuals for these tasks. They come with the package! Second, the missions that begin with a core group have a high degree of success. Few of them fail to develop into churches.

Perhaps I should mention two possible disadvantages as well. First, the church that begins with a core group usually clones the mother church. If the mission is planted in a community much different from that of the mother church, the new church may need to take a different approach. In this case, cloning the mother church is a disadvantage. A second possible disadvantage of this model is that malcontents often volunteer to join the core group. They want to join the new church to get away from the mother church. The church planter must be careful not to transplant problems from the mother church into the mission congregation. This second problem can be avoided if the members of the core group are prayerfully chosen.

Sunday School

Through the years many churches have been started by establishing Sunday schools. In this method, workers start a Sunday school in hope that it will develop into a church. This method is less used nowadays than in the past.

Revival

Many denominations start new churches with revival meetings. Often these groups use a tent, temporary structure, or rented hall to house the meetings. The evangelist holds nightly services for some weeks. As people are saved, the evangelist disciples the believers. When the group is large enough, the evangelist organizes the members of the group into a church. Assemblies of God missionaries used this method to good effect in the Philippines in the 1980s.

Institutional

A number of churches have been established throughout the world in connection with Christian institutions. For example, a university church may arise out of a ministry to college students. Or, a church might develop on the campus of a mission hospital. Normally, the church is a spin-off from an institution that was founded to meet another need. However, sometimes the institution is established with the hope that it will provide a beachhead for evangelism and church planting. This has been the case with many mission hospitals.

Lay Agreement

Sometimes churches are planted by laypersons who move into an unchurched community. They agree among themselves that a church is needed, and they take the initiative to organize the church.

Pioneer

Pioneer church planting is much the same as the cross-cultural growth described in chapter 2. There is no mother church close by. The denomination or missions agency sends in a church planter to start the work from scratch. The church planter does surveys and advertising to discover interested persons. Then the church planter starts fellowship Bible study groups. People are saved and baptized. The group grows and begins conducting worship services. Eventually the group constitutes as a church. The pioneer church planter may stay to pastor the church or, more commonly, go on to another place to start another church.

Denominational Sponsorship

Often associations, synods, or church districts decide to sponsor a new church or churches. They employ a church planter or solicit churches in their area to sponsor a new church. The Dallas Baptist Association in Texas has developed a successful strategy for starting churches in new areas. An associational staff member monitors new housing developments around the city. When a new area is planned, the association buys property in the new subdivision while the land is less expensive. The association holds the land until houses and schools are built. Then the association solicits one or more neighboring churches to sponsor the new mission. As you might expect, this method has worked very well, but it requires funds for strategic land acquisition.

Satellite Churches

One of the most popular methods today, both in North America and around the world, is the satellite approach. New congregations formed by this approach are semiautonomous. They meet weekly on their own, but they maintain an organic relationship with the mother church. They function like annexes or branches of the mother church. The pastor of the mother church supervises the pastors or leaders of the satellite congregations. Some of these eventually become independent churches, while others don't. Ordinarily this is not a great concern. The main thing is to reach people for Christ and minister to them. Satellite churches often minister to people who are very different from the members of the mother church. The members of satellite churches should not be kept away from the mother church; they may participate in many activities at the mother church. The point is to take the gospel where these people live.

Multicongregational Churches

Some urban churches are composed of several different ethnic congregations. They share the same building, cost of utilities, and staff members. Leaders from the different congregations join to form a church council that handles the church's affairs. The financial advantages of planting churches of this type are obvious. Also obvious is the need for patience and cooperation in making these arrangements work.

Traditional Church Extension

Through the years most churches have been planted by existing churches located nearby. This is a good method. Churches should give birth to churches. Paul planted churches of Asia Minor and

Greece, expecting that these churches would become seedbed churches. He hoped the gospel would flow from these cities into the surrounding countryside. Apparently, his method worked very well (1 Thess. 1:8). New churches typically pass through six stages:[9]

1. *Discovery Stage.* The mother church locates a community or group that needs a new church. The church does research to discover the characteristics of the community and its needs.

2. *Preparation Stage.* Leaders of the mother church prepare the sponsoring church for the task ahead. This involves preaching, teaching, and researching. The pastor preaches and teaches about church planting. The missions committee (or council) prepares a proposal for the church that explains where and how the new church will be started.

3. *Cultivation Stage.* Those involved in planting the new church will cultivate relationships with the people in the target community. This cultivation may include surveys, visitation, and various types of appealing activities.

4. *Fellowship Stage.* The church planter begins holding fellowship Bible studies. The Bible studies win people to Christ and help the people bond together into a group.

5. *Mission Stage.* The new mission begins holding regular worship services. The mission organizes a graded Sunday school and begins to collect offerings. The church planter begins to train people to assume positions of leadership in the mission.

6. *Church Stage.* The mission is constituted as an autonomous church. No longer is it a mission, dependent on the mother church for money or guidance. The new church takes its place as a separate member of the denomination at various levels. At this stage the new church should begin looking for a place to plant a daughter church. The church planter must train the members of the new church to develop "church growth eyes," and must help the people recognize opportunities for church planting around them.

SUMMARY

Church planting is an effective method of evangelism. By starting new congregations, existing churches can evangelize unreached groups and areas. Church leaders should view church planting as an essential type of church growth.

When churches plant daughter churches, they follow the early church's example, obey the Great Commission, and enhance their growth potential. Furthermore, new churches grow more rapidly than older churches; new churches baptize more persons proportionately than older churches; new churches replace churches that die; and new churches minister to new housing developments. Normally, a new church is the best way to reach the ethnic groups in a community. New churches are also needed to reach new generations. Baby boomers and baby busters prefer to worship in ways different from their parents and grandparents, and new churches can provide the alternative styles of worship that are appealing to them. Finally, denominations cannot grow (or even maintain their size) without church planting. Denominations that aggressively plant churches grow; those that don't decline.

Some people raise objections to church planting. The three main objections are: it costs too much, we have enough churches already, and we don't want to offend existing churches. Some types of church planting are expensive, but there are methods that cost less. A few areas are overchurched, but most areas need more churches. Existing churches often overlook specific groups of people in their communities. Some pastors might object when a new church is planted in their area; however, a face-to-face meeting may reassure them that no sheep will be stolen.

There are many different approaches to church planting. Perhaps the most common are the core group model and the traditional church extension. In the core group model, a group of members from the mother church leave the church to form the nucleus of a daughter church. In the traditional model, the members of the church missions committee take the lead in choosing a place for the new church, and they find a church planter to direct the effort. The main thing in choosing a model is to choose the one that best fits the circumstances.

Churches that plant daughter churches receive many benefits. Usually, the mother church experiences growth along with the daughter church. The mother church finds satisfaction and fulfillment when the new church is organized. God blesses obedient congregations; and when a church plants a daughter church, God blesses the church in many ways. Finally, new church development contributes much to denominational health and vitality.

STUDY QUESTIONS

1. In your opinion, what are the three most important reasons for planting new churches?

2. Why do new churches grow more rapidly than older churches?

3. What group or area in your community needs a new church? Which model of church planting would work best in that community situation?

4. What are three benefits that come from church planting?

5. What are the three most significant objections to church planting? How would you answer these objections?

6. What are the six stages involved in planting a church through traditional church extension?

FOR FURTHER STUDY

Brock, Charles. *Indigenous Church Planting: A Practical Journey.* Neosho, Mo.: Church Growth International, 1994.

Lewis, Larry L. *The Church Planter's Handbook.* Nashville: Broadman Press, 1992.

Malphurs, Aubrey. *Planting Growing Churches.* Grand Rapids: Baker Book House, 1992.

Ratliff, Joe S. and Michael J. Cox. *Church Planting in the African-American Community.* Nashville: Broadman Press, 1993.

Romo, Oscar I. *American Mosaic: Church Planting in Ethnic America.* Nashville: Broadman Press, 1993.

Tidsworth, Floyd Jr. *Life Cycle of a New Congregation.* Nashville: Broadman Press, 1992.

Wagner, C. Peter. *Church Planting for a Greater Harvest.* Ventura, Calif.: Regal Books, 1990).

ENDNOTES

CHAPTER 1

1. Delos Miles, "The Lordship of Christ: Implications for Evangelism," *Southwestern Journal of Theology* (Spring 1991): 45.

2. Delos Miles, *Master Principles of Evangelism* (Nashville: Broadman Press, 1982), 32; see also John Mark Terry, *Evangelism: A Concise History* (Nashville: Broadman & Holman, 1994), 6–8.

CHAPTER 2

1. C. Kirk Hadaway, *Church Growth Principles* (Nashville: Broadman Press, 1991), 163.

2. Thom Rainer, *Giant Awakenings* (Nashville: Broadman & Holman, 1995), 23.

3. Ken Hemphill, *The Antioch Effect* (Nashville: Broadman & Holman, 1994), 61.

4. Ibid.

5. R. A. Pegram, "Church Growth Through Intercessory Prayer," *Good News* (September/October 1995): 24.

6. I first learned the ACTS approach when I studied *MasterLife* by Avery Willis, published by The Baptist Sunday School Board, 127 Ninth Avenue North, Nashville, Tennessee 37234.

7. *SBC Life,* January 1995, 3.

8. Available through the Evangelism Department of the Baptist General Convention of Texas.

9. Orville Scott, "Texans Rediscovering the Power of Prayer," *The Baptist Standard* (September 21, 1994): 11.

10. Ibid., 10.

11. Irma Duke, "God Still Breaks Down Barriers," *Alabama Baptist* (July 22, 1993): 12.

12. Earle E. Cairns, *An Endless Line of Splendor* (Wheaton: Tyndale House, 1986), 340.

13. J. Edwin Orr, "The Role of Prayer in Spiritual Awakening," *Campus Crusade for Christ*, 1976, 1.

14. Ibid., 6.

15. Larry Wynn, "Something Different Is Happening in Dacula," *Growing Churches* (Winter 1996): 44–45.

CHAPTER 3

1. Thom Rainer, *The Book of Church Growth* (Nashville: Broadman Press, 1993), 20.

2. C. Peter Wagner, *Your Church Can Grow* (Ventura: Calif.: Regal Books, 1976), 14.

3. Lewis A. Drummond, *Leading Your Church in Evangelism* (Nashville: Broadman Press, 1975), 21.

4. For a more thorough discussion of the relationship between evangelism and church growth, see C. Peter Wagner, "Evangelism and the Church Growth Movement," in Thom S. Rainer, ed., *Evangelism in the Twenty-First Century* (Wheaton: Harold Shaw, 1989).

5. Rick Warren, *The Purpose Driven Church* (Grand Rapids: Zondervan Publishing House, 1995), 17.

6. Wagner, *Your Church Can Grow,* 106.

7. Warren, *The Purpose Driven Church,* 49.

8. Gene Mims, *Kingdom Principles for Church Growth* (Nashville: Convention Press, 1994), 108.

9. Ibid., 39.

10. Ibid., 44.

11. Ibid., 50.

12. Ibid., 57.

13. For help in this area, see Robert Dale, *To Dream Again* (Nashville: Broadman Press, 1981).

14. For more information about hindrances, see these two articles: Jerry Shreveland, "Why Churches Plateau," *Indiana Baptist* (February 15, 1994): 14; and Jerry Sutton, "Why Are Churches Not Growing?" *Southern Baptist Communicator* (June 1990): 18.

15. Ken Hemphill, "Characteristics of Effective Churches," *Missions USA* (July-August 1994): 63. Hemphill develops these ideas more fully in his book, *The Antioch Effect* (Nashville: Broadman & Holman, 1994).

16. Warren, *The Purpose Driven Church,* 31.

CHAPTER 4

1. "Busters to Dictate Booming Church Changes?" *Word and Way* (August 1995): 9.

2. Win Arn, "Paradigms: Are They Working for You or Against You?" *Growing Churches* (April 1992): 12.

3. David A. Roozen and C. Kirk Hadaway, *Church and Denominational Growth* (Nashville: Abingdon Press, 1993), 39.

4. Arn, "Paradigms," 12.

5. Warren, *The Purpose Driven Church,* 63.

6. Most of the material following comes from Mark Terry, "Proactive Leadership," *Growing Churches* (Winter 1995): 29–30.

CHAPTER 5

1. Win Arn, *The Pastor's Manual for Effective Ministry* (Monrovia, Calif.: Church Growth, 1988), 43.

2. As you organize your council, you would do well to use the *Church Evangelism Council Manual,* published by the Home Mission Board of the Southern Baptist Convention. It is quite helpful, and best of all, it's free.

3. Burt Nanus, *Visionary Leadership* (San Francisco: Jossey-Bass, 1992), 8.

4. George Barna, *The Power of Vision* (Ventura, Calif.: Regal Books, 1992), 28.

5. Rick Warren, *The Purpose Driven Church* (Grand Rapids: Zondervan Publishing House, 1995), 107.

6. Barna, *The Power of Vision,* 35–36.

7. Quoted in Rick Warren, *The Purpose Driven Church,* 77–79.

8. Paul Powell, *Building an Evangelistic Church* (Dallas: Annuity Board, 1991), 29–33.

9. Ibid., 12.

10. Warren, *The Purpose Driven Church,* 160–65.

11. Lyle E. Schaller, *Parish Planning* (Nashville: Abingdon, 1971), 95.

12. Ibid., 162.

13. Ibid., 178.

14. Calvin Ratz, *Mastering Outreach and Evangelism* (Portland: Multnomah Press, 1990), 41–43.

15. Warren, *The Purpose Driven Church,* 185–200.

16. Powell, *Building an Evangelistic Church,* 12.

17. Ron Shrum, "Goal Setting and Church Growth," *Growing Churches* (January/February 1992): 28.

18. "Evangelism Ideas for Every Month of the Year," *Growing Churches* (January-March 1993): 49.

CHAPTER 6

1. Stephen Neill, *The History of Christian Missions* (New York: Penguin Books, 1986), 46–47.

2. Neil Jackson Jr., "Motivation for Personal Visitation," in Harry Piland, ed., *Going . . . One on One* (Nashville: Convention Press, 1994), 37.

3. Kenneth Gangel, *Feeding and Leading* (Wheaton: Victor Books, 1989), 168–169.

4. Ibid., 39.

5. John Bisagno, *How to Build an Evangelistic Church* (Nashville: Broadman Press, 1971), 24–26.

6. Calvin Ratz, *Mastering Outreach and Evangelism* (Portland: Multnomah Press, 1990), 68–69.

7. Robert Coleman, *The Master Plan of Evangelism* (Old Tappan, N.J.: Fleming H. Revell Co., 1963), 6; see also Ken Hemphill, *The Antioch Effect* (Nashville: Broadman & Holman, 1994), 86–87.

8. The Home Mission Board of the Southern Baptist Convention offers a program called "The One-Day Soul Winning Workshop." This seminar can be accomplished in six or seven hours, and it teaches members to share their testimonies using witnessing booklets.

CHAPTER 7

1. "Millions Finding Care and Support in Small Groups," *Emerging Trends* (October 1994): 2–5.

2. Kennon Callahan, *Twelve Keys to an Effective Church* (San Francisco: HarperCollins, 1983), 35.

3. Callahan, *Twelve Keys,* 36–37.

4. J. Mark Terry, "Growing Through Groups," *Growing Churches* (October-December 1994), 42.

5. Ralph Neighbour Jr., *Where Do We Go from Here: A Guidebook for the Cell Group Church* (Houston: Touch Publications, 1990), 20–22.

6. Ibid., 24.

7. Carl F. George, *Prepare Your Church for the Future* (Grand Rapids: Fleming Revell Company, 1991), 214–15.

8. Ken Hemphill, "Weaknesses to Some Current Approaches," *Growing Churches* (July-September 1994): 63–64.

9. Charles Arn, "Small Groups . . . Ally or Adversary," *Ministry Advantage* (November-December 1993): 5–6.

10. George Hunter, *To Spread the Power* (Nashville: Abingdon Press, 1989), 128.

11. Carl F. George, "Innovations in Evangelism," in *Leadership Handbooks of Practical Theology,* vol. 2, (Grand Rapids: Baker Book House, 1994), 50.

12. Pat Cole, "Preaching, Sunday School, Prayer Cited for Growth," *Western Recorder* (12 December 1995): 6.

13. Marv Knox, "Best Evangelism Tool?" *Western Recorder* (28 May 1991): 3.

14. Larry Lewis, *Organize to Evangelize* (Nashville: Broadman Press, 1988), 22–30.

15. C. Kirk Hadaway, *Church Growth Principles* (Nashville: Broadman Press, 1991), 40–42.

CHAPTER 8

1. Larry Lewis, *Organize to Evangelize* (Nashville: Broadman Press, 1988), 31.

2. Kevin E. Ruffcorn, *Rural Evangelism* (Minneapolis: Augsburg Press, 1994), 57.

3. George Hunter, *The Contagious Congregation* (Nashville: Abingdon, 1978), 96.

4. Larry Gilbert, *Team Evangelism* (Lynchburg, Va.: Church Growth Institute, 1991), 66–67.

5. Darrell W. Robinson, *Total Church Life* (Nashville: Broadman Press, 1993), 159–62.

6. Rick Warren, *The Purpose Driven Church* (Grand Rapids: Zondervan Publishing House, 1996), 189.

7. Chip Alford, "Velcro-ize to Reach Prospects," *Facts and Trends* (November 1995): 8.

CHAPTER 9

1. Ronald K. Brown, "A Definition of Personal Visitation," in *Going . . . One on One,* ed. Harry M. Piland (Nashville: Convention Press, 1994), 21.

2. Larry L. Lewis, *Organize to Evangelize* (Nashville: Broadman Press, 1988), 55.

3. See Kennon Callahan, *Twelve Keys to an Effective Church* (New York: Harper-Collins Publishers, 1983); Lyle Schaller, *Parish Planning* (Nashville: Abingdon Press, 1983), 214; William H. Hinson, *A Place to Dig In* (Nashville: Abingdon Press, 1987), 113; Paul Powell, *The Nuts and Bolts of Church Growth* (Nashville: Broadman Press, 1982), 49.

4. C. Kirk Hadaway, *Church Growth Principles* (Nashville: Broadman, 1991), 21–22.

5. Christopher Jay Johnson, "A Plan of Visitation for the First Baptist Church, Russell, Kentucky" (D.Min. Project Report, The Southern Baptist Theological Seminary, 1993).

6. Larry Gilbert, *Team Evangelism* (Lynchburg, Va.: Church Growth Institute), 103. This is Gilbert's adaptation of the famous Engel Scale.

7. Ibid., 95.

8. John Savage, *The Apathetic and Bored Church Member* (Reynoldsburg, Ohio: L.E.A.D. Consultants, 1976), 79.

9. Lewis, *Organize to Evangelize,* 56; Hadaway, *Church Growth Principles,* 23.

10. Paul Powell, *Building an Evangelistic Church* (Dallas: Annuity Board, 1991), 44.

11. Herb Miller, *How to Build a Magnetic Church* (Nashville: Abingdon Press, 1987), 72.

CHAPTER 10

1. Gary McIntosh and Glen Martin, *Finding Them, Keeping Them* (Nashville: Broadman Press, 1992), 22.

2. Lyle Schaller, *The Seven-Day-a-Week Church* (Nashville: Abingdon Press, 1992), 48, 51.

3. Brian Smith, "The 7-Day Church," *Word and Way* (August 10, 1995): 4.

4. Larry Lewis, *Organize to Evangelize* (Nashville: Broadman Press, 1988), 100.

5. "VBS Still One of the Best Outreach Tools," *Western Recorder* (Feb. 15, 1994): 1–A.

6. Quoted in Delos Miles, *Evangelism and Social Involvement* (Nashville: Broadman Press, 1986), 7.

7. Donald Atkinson and Charles Roesel, *Meeting Needs/Sharing Christ* (Nashville: Convention Press, 1995), 10.

8. Delos Miles, "Church Social Work and Evangelism as Partners," in Thom S. Rainer, ed., *Evangelism in the Twenty-First Century* (Wheaton: Harold Shaw Publishers, 1989), 57.

9. Atkinson and Roesel, *Meeting Needs,* 74.

10. Michael Chute, "If You Minister, They Will Come," *SBC Life* (December 1995): 6.

11. Ibid.

12. Elton Trueblood, *The Company of the Committed* (New York: Harper & Row, 1961), 53.

13. Orville Scott, "Wilshire Overwhelmed by Ministry Response," *Baptist Standard* (March 2, 1994): 13.

14. Bonnie Steffen, "Tillie the Texas Tornado," *Christianity Today* (October 4, 1993): 12–13.

15. Ferris Jordan, "Aging in America: A Ministry Frontier," *Growing Disciples* (July-September 1995), 5–10.

16. Kenneth Quick, "Good Sports: Keeping Your Church's Recreational Ministry in Bounds," *Leadership* (Winter 1996): 101.

CHAPTER 11

1. William Easum, *The Church Growth Handbook* (Nashville: Abingdon Press, 1990), 43.

2. Kennon Callahan, *Twelve Keys to an Effective Church* (San Francisco: Harper and Row, 1983), 24.

3. Barna Research Group Report, "The Church Today: Insightful Statistics and Commentary" (Glendale, Calif.), 46.

4. Chevis Horne, "The Pastor as a Leader of Worship," *The Baptist Program* (November 1988), 11.

5. James Emery White, *Opening the Front Door: Worship and Church Growth* (Nashville: Convention Press, 1992), 156–57.

6. W. T. Conner, *The Gospel of Redemption* (Nashville: Broadman Press, 1945), 277.

7. White, *Opening the Front Door,* 50.

8. Rick Warren, *The Purpose-Driven Church* (Grand Rapids: Zondervan Publishing House, 1995), 198–99.

9. David A. Roozen and C. Kirk Hadaway, *Church and Denominational Growth* (Nashville: Abingdon Press, 1993), 129.

10. C. Kirk Hadaway, *Church Growth Principles* (Nashville: Broadman Press, 1991), 70.

11. Hadaway, *Church Growth Principles,* 72.

12. Warren, *The Purpose Driven Church,* 245.

13. Glen Martin, Seminar: "Designing a Worship Service to Reach the Unchurched."

14. Warren, *The Purpose Driven Church,* 302–303.

15. James Emery White, "Preaching That Reaches People," *Proclaim* (January 1994): 46.

16. John R. Bisagno, *How to Build an Evangelistic Church* (Nashville: Broadman Press, 1971), 75–88.

17. William Easum, *Church Growth Handbook* (Nashville: Abingdon Press, 1990), 51.

18. Bill Hybels, "Speaking to the Secular Mind," *Leadership* (Summer 1988): 1.

19. Ed Dobson, *Starting a Seeker-Sensitive Service* (Grand Rapids: Zondervan Publishing House, 1993), 18.

20. Thom Rainer, *The Book of Church Growth* (Nashville: Broadman Press, 1993), 235.

CHAPTER 12

1. Joey Faucette, "Which Way Do I Go? Advertising Do's and Don'ts for Churches," *Growing Churches* (January-March 1993): 50–51.

2. Ibid.

3. Tom Cheyney, "Seven Sins of Church Advertising," *The Baptist Messenger* (22 June 1995): 12.

4. Robert Screen, "Effective Communication to Your Community," in Win Arn, ed., *The Pastor's Church Growth Handbook,* vol. 1 (Pasadena: Church Growth Press, 1979), 206–207.

5. Faucette, "Which Way Do I Go?" 51.

6. Ibid.

7. Ibid.

8. Ed Litton, "Reaching the Unreachable Through Direct Mail," *Growing Churches* (January-March 1993): 13.

9. Ibid., 14–15.

10. Quoted in C. C. Risenhoover, "Pastor Says What Works in Television Is Preaching," *Beam International* (Winter 1996): 6.

11. Darrell Robinson, "Why Converts Come to Christ," *Missions USA* (July-August 1995), 18.

12. Jeffrey K. Hadden and Charles Swann, *Prime Time Preachers* (Reading, Mass.: Addison-Wesley Publishing Co., 1981), 61–62.

13. Delos Miles, *Introduction to Evangelism* (Nashville: Broadman Press, 1983), 280.

14. Quoted in C. C. Risenhoover, "Pastor Says Media Should Not Be the Tail That Wags the Dog," *Beam International* (Winter 1996), 8.

15. Ibid.

CHAPTER 13

1. Mark Wingfield, "Barna: Old Is New in Good Evangelism," *Western Recorder* (February 27, 1996): 10.

2. Todd Deaton, "Change–Vital for a Growing Congregation," *Biblical Recorder* (March 23, 1996): 3.

3. Dale Wicker, "Practical Ideas for Event Evangelism," *Growing Churches* (April-June 1992): 60.

4. Thom S. Rainer, *Effective Evangelistic Churches* (Nashville: Broadman & Holman, 1996), 32.

5. Richard H. Harris, *Revival Planbook for the Local Church* (Atlanta: Home Mission Board, 1993), 17.

6. The *Revival Planbook* published by the Home Mission Board of the Southern Baptist Convention contains job descriptions and check lists for committees and other helpful information.

7. The *Decision Time* materials published by the Baptist Sunday School Board (127 Ninth Avenue North, Nashville, Tenn. 37234) are an excellent resource for training counselors.

8. Resources for planning and training follow-up workers include the Home Mission Board's booklet, "Follow-up Guide for Local Church Revival;" and "Living in Christ," a booklet prepared by the Billy Graham Evangelistic Association.

9. Thom S. Rainer, *Effective Evangelistic Churches: Successful Churches Reveal What Works and What Doesn't* (Nashville: Broadman & Holman, 1996), 33.

10. This acrostic comes from Thad Hamilton, *Special Evangelistic Events* (Atlanta: Home Mission Board, 1994), 7.

11. Ibid.

12. Rick Warren, *The Purpose Driven Church* (Grand Rapids: Zondervan Publishing House, 1995), 142.

13. Dale Wicker, "Practical Ideas for Event Evangelism," *Growing Churches* (April-June 1992): 60–61.

CHAPTER 14

1. Mark S. Jones, *Reclaiming Inactive Church Members* (Nashville: Broadman Press, 1988), 9.

2. Ibid.

3. Robert Jeamby, "Why New Members Don't Stay," *Western Recorder* (July 4, 1995), 3.

4. James Hightower, *After They Join* (Nashville: Convention Press, 1995), 61–62.

5. Roland Q. Leavell, *The Romance of Evangelism* (New York: Fleming H. Revell Co., 1942): 89.

6. Waylon B. Moore, *Multiplying Disciples* (Tampa: Missions Unlimited, 1981), 21–22.

7. Waylon B. Moore, *New Testament Follow-up* (Grand Rapids: Eerdmans Publishing Co., 1963), 23–27.

8. Ibid., 29–36.

9. Moore, *Multiplying Disciples,* 51–99.

10. Moore, *New Testament Follow-up,* 37–44.

11. *Follow-up Guide for Local Church Revival* (Atlanta: Home Mission Board) and the training notebook *Decision Time* (Nashville: Baptist Sunday School Board) provide guidance on training follow-up workers.

12. Lyle E. Schaller, *Assimilating New Members* (Nashville: Abingdon Press, 1978), 16.

13. The "Encourager Plan" was developed by the Baptist Sunday School Board.

14. Joyce Martin, "Pleasant View Keeps New Members in the Pew," *Western Recorder* (July 4, 1995): 3.

15. Rick Warren, *The Purpose Driven Church* (Grand Rapids: Zondervan Publishing House, 1995), 315–16.

16. Ibid., 315–16.

17. Ibid., 318.

18. See Timothy George, ed., *Baptist Confessions, Covenants, and Catechisms,* The Library of Baptist Classics (Nashville: Broadman & Holman Publishers, 1996).

19. Donald Atkinson and Charles Roesel, *Meeting Needs/Sharing Christ* (Nashville: Convention Press, 1995), 84.

20. Ibid., 86–87.

CHAPTER 15

1. C. Peter Wagner, *Church Planting for a Greater Harvest* (Ventura, Calif.: Regal Books, 1990), 33.

2. Charles Chaney, "New Churches and the Unsaved," *MissionsUSA* (January-February 1995): 12.

3. David Roozen and C. Kirk Hadaway, *Church and Denominational Growth* (Nashville: Abingdon Press, 1993), 80.

4. C. Kirk Hadaway, "The Impact of New Church Development on Southern Baptist Growth," *Review of Religious Research* 31 (June 1990): 377–78.

5. Win Arn, *The Pastor's Manual for Effective Ministry* (Monrovia, Calif.: Church Growth, 1988), 41, 16.

6. Lyle Schaller, *44 Steps Up Off the Plateau* (Nashville: Abingdon Press, 1993), 47.

7. *Guide for Planting New Churches* (Atlanta: Home Mission Board, 1991), 17.

8. Bonnie Steffen, "Tillie, the Texas Tornado," *Christianity Today* (October 4, 1993): 12–13; "Church Growth Expert Holds Dialogue On-Line," *Western Recorder* (January 3, 1995), 2.

9. The Southern Baptist Home Mission Board has described the steps involved in church extension in its helpful publication, *Guide for Planting Churches.* This guide is available free of charge from the Home Mission Board.

INDEX

➤ ———————— ◄